W. HOCK HOCHHEIM'S

HAND, STICK, KNIFE, GUN
CLOSE QUARTER COMBATIVES

TRAINING MISSION THREE

CQCG

THE HOCHHEIM GROUP

CLOSE QUARTER COMBAT GROUP
TRAINING MISSION THREE

by W. Hock Hochheim

WARNINGS!

TRAINING MISSION THREE

Table of Contents

1) The CQC Group:
    Overview/Review — Page 8

2) Unarmed Combatives
    UC Strike 3: The Forearm Module — Page 11
    UC Kick 3: The Knee Module — Page 31
    UC Takedown 3: The Rear Takedowns Module — Page 37

3) SDMS Impact Weapon Combatives
    SDMS/Stick Level 3: The DMS Combat Module — Page 44

4) Knife/Counter-Knife Combatives
    Knife Level 3: The Reverse Grip Slash Module — Page 68

5) Gun/Counter-Gun Combatives
    Gun Level 3: The Arrest, Control, Restain and Contain Module — Page 94

For information about testing requirements, email Hock @Hock@hockscqc.com

CQCG Course Review

CQCG Training Mission Progression Overview:
All training is expressed in a *Modular Concept.* A module includes learning the basic execution of a particular tactic, troubleshooting common counters to the tactic, skill and flow drill development of the tactic, counters and using the tactic in standing, kneeling and ground positions, fighting against unarmed, stick, knife and gun weaponry. The bold/highlighted levels appear in this book.

CQCG Unarmed Combatives

The Strike Modules
Level 1	The Finger Strike Module
Level 2	The Palm Strike Module
Level 3	**The Forearm Strike Module**
Level 4	The Hammer Fist Module
Level 5	Fistfight! The Punch/Counter-Punch Strike Module
Level 6	The Elbow Strike Module
Level 7	The Body Ram Module
Level 8	The Limited Use of the Head Butt Module
Level 9	The Strike/Block/Counter-Strike Module
Level 10	The Combat Scenario Performance Module

The Kick Modules
Level 1	The Frontal Snap Kick Module
Level 2	The Stomp Kick Module
Level 3	**The Knee Strike Module**
Level 4	The Rear Leg Round Kick Module
Level 5	The Front Leg Hook Kick Module
Level 6	The Back Kick Module
Level 7	The Side Kick Module
Level 8	The Front Thrust Module
Level 9	The Counters to Kicks Module
Level 10	The Combat Scenario Performance Module

The Takedowns and Throws Modules (these include joint crank studies)
Level 1	The Finger Attack Takedowns Module
Level 2	The Circular/Wheel Takedowns Module
Level 3	**The Rear Takedowns Module**
Level 4	The Bent and Straight Arm Takedowns Module
Level 5	The Front Takedowns Module
Level 6	The Neck Attack Takedowns Module
Level 7	The Push/Pull Takedowns Module
Level 8	The Tackle Takedowns Module
Level 9	The Leg Attack Takedowns Module
Level 10	The Combat Scenario Performance Module

CQCG Knife/Counter-Knife Course

Level 1	Knife Introduction and Quick Draw Combat Module
Level 2	The Saber Grip Slash Knife Module
Level 3	**Reverse Grip Slash Knife Module**
Level 4	The Saber Grip Hacking Module and Spartan Module
Level 5	The Reverse Grip Knife Stabbing Module
Level 6	The Saber Grip Stabbing Module and Chain of the Knife Module
Level 7	The Pommel Strike and Closed Folder Strike Module
Level 8	In The Clutches of Module
Level 9	Unarmed Vs. the Knife Combat Module
Level 10	The Knife/Counter-Knife Combat Scenario Module

CQCG SDMS (Single and Double-handed grip) Impact Weapon Course

Level 1	The SDMS Introduction and Quick Draw Combat Module
Level 2	The SMS Solo-Hand Grip Command and Mastery Module
Level 3	**The DMS Double-Hand Grip Command and Mastery Module**
Level 4	The SDMS CQC Block and Strike Combat Module
Level 5	The SDMS Weapon Disarms and Retention Combat Module
Level 6	The DMS Pull Grappling Series: Combat Module
Level 7	The DMS Push Grappling Series: Combat Module
Level 8	The DMS Turn Grappling Series: Combat Module
Level 9	The Unarmed Combatives versus SDMS Attacks Module
Level 10	The SDMS Combat Scenarios Module

CQCG Gun/Counter-Gun Course

Level 1	The Quick Draw Combat Module
Level 2	The Walking Point/Search Module
Level 3	**The Control, Restrain and Contain Arrest and Capture Module**
Level 4	The Pistol Disarm and Retention Combat Module
Level 5	The Long Gun Disarm and Retention Module
Level 6	The Shoot/Move/Cover Module
Level 7	Emergency! The Tactical Medicine and Fight While Wounded Module
Level 8	The Pistol Instructor Module
Level 9	The Shotgun Instructor Module
Level 10	The Gun Combat Scenarios Module

CQCG Level 3
Level 3 consists of all the level 3 material within each hand, stick, knife and gun category.

CQC Group Rank and Instructorships
Various rankings in each or all the courses can be achieved in seminars and classes. Train with us and master these courses. CQCG Instructorships involve classroom training, hands-on practice and both written and physical testing in a designated camp or course.

> *Basic CQCG Instructor*   *upon completing Level 3*
> *Advanced CQCG Instructor*   *upon completing Level 6*
> *Expertise CQCG Instructor*   *upon completing Level 9*
> *Master CQCG Instructor*   *upon completing Level 10*

Re-certification
As always, you must maintain proper ethical and moral standards. You cannot be a criminal or be attached to any radical or questionable organization of this or any other nation. I need to know that you are continuing to work out, teach, learn and grow. I need to see you in a training session at least once every 12 months for continued re-certification. These are the standards I demand.

My Training Promise to You
Civilian and martial arts courses are almost always off-base with real world needs and unplugged from the newest, scientific trends to combat enemy soldiers, terrorists and criminals. Martial arts dynasties must be perpetuated. Traditions must be upheld. Military and police academies must spend time with political and non-combat related training agendas. SEALS need to swim. Rangers and Recon need to reconnoiter. Berets must master commo. Police need to understand traffic accident reporting. The list of non-combat training subject requirements for these groups is almost endless. There are classes on saluting, organized hazing and harassment, marching, etc. that subtract precious time from specific combatives study. Even courses designated as combat courses waste time on jumping jacks, marching and other steps to develop physical fitness. A true warrior is fit, comes fit and remains fit on his own time. As a result, 100 hours of training may have only 40 hours of actual combat tactics.

The CQC Group training mission books, this being the third of 10 books, will set forth comprehensive and insightful training doctrine and methods unlike any other. We bridge the gap between the military, the police, the martial artist and the aware citizenry. I have interfaced with many members of these groups around the world. I am convinced that this CQC course is the most comprehensive, complete, scientific, hand, stick, knife and gun, close quarters course in the world, bar none. Anywhere. This is my promise. Best of the best, forged from the best disciplines.

Epiphany.
It is all here for you already.
Are you ready for the next step?

Unarmed Combatives
Strike 3: The Forearm Strike Attack Module

The Forearm Strike Overview

The forearm strike is favored by many military, police and street survival experts. The forearms have long been nicknamed the "lead pipes" of the body. The ulna bones are thick and are not easily hurt or injured. You can use all four sides as a striking surface.

Forearm Strike Studies and Observations 1) Forearm Strike Delivery

The forearm strike may be delivered in a thrusting manner or a hooking manner.

> Forearm Strike 1) A thrusting power strike
> Forearm Strike 2) A hooking strike

A thrusting forearm strike.

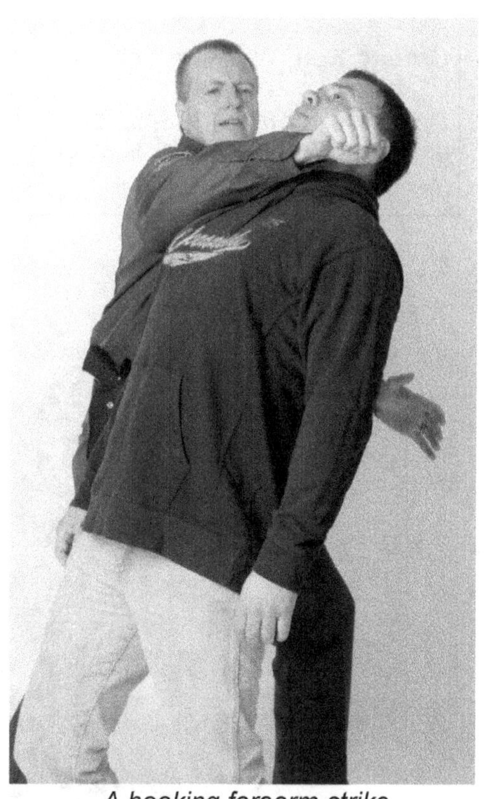

A hooking forearm strike.

Forearm Strike Studies and Observations 2) Body Synergy

Biomechanics experts and sports coaches dissect ways to produce maximum performance. In this vein, the palm strike must be executed with full body support when possible. Hip and shoulder rotation, proper balance and relaxation, with sudden explosiveness all contribute to success.

Forearm Strike Studies and Observations 3) Both ends help the middle

If the forearm strike is a little close, then it becomes a handy elbow strike. Should the chaos of the combat take you a bit too far from the target, then the forearm strike can become a hammer fist.

Forearm Strike Studies and Observations Training Methodologies

Solo Command and Mastery- As shown in *Training Mission One*, the Clock Drill is one of our training methods. Create body synergy with practice in the air.

Striking Drills- Develop goal-specific strength, target acquisition and resistance experience with pad, mitt, wooden or padded posts and heavy bag drills.

Statue Drills- As first shown in *Training Mission One*, the Statue Drills are also our main training methods, especially for beginners. For a complete breakdown of the skill drill, please refer back to *Training Mission One.*

Skill Drills- We introduce at least one skill/flow drill to develop superior execution. Do not obsess on multitudes of skill drills, obsess instead on combative applications.

Clinch Drill- We will work the tactic through the common body crash and clinch of opponents.

Ground Roll- We will work the tactic through the common ground fight positions.

Option Awareness Combat Scenarios- We will *crisis-rehearse* the tactics in standing, kneeling and ground combat scenarios fighting against hands, sticks, knives and guns.

The statue drill is an important foundation to help define the options of striking.

The Forearm Strike Synergy Solo Command and Mastery

Practice these first in the air so that you can learn the orientations and the proper body synergy. Step forward and twist your torso with each strike to enhance balance and power.

The Thrusting Forearm Strike Solo Command and Mastery

The right arm thrusting forearm strike.

The left arm thrusting forearm strike.

The Hooking Forearm Strike Solo Command and Mastery

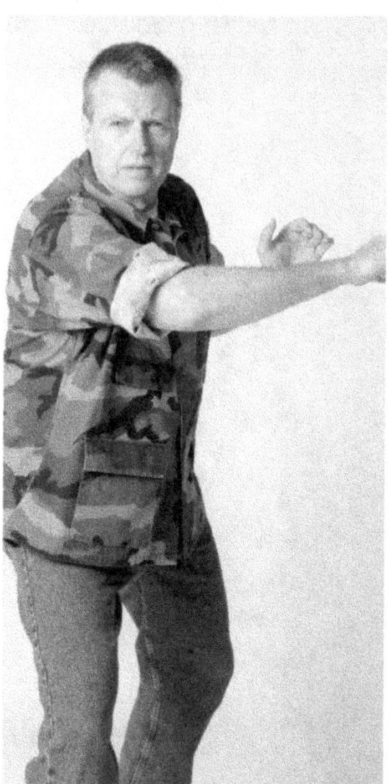

12 o'clock hooking fore-arm strike, from high.

3 o'clock hooking forearm strike, from the right.

6 o'clock hooking forearm strike, from below.

9 o'clock hooking fore-arm strike, from the left.

The Strikes

1) The Top-side, or 12 o'clock hooking strike.
2) The right side, or 3 o'clock hooking strike.
3) The low, or 6 o'clock hooking strike.
4) The left-side, or 9 o'clock hooking strike.
5) The center strikes, or axis clock thrust strikes.

The Practice

1) Practice with right and left hands.
2) Practice with free and easy moving footwork.
3) Practice knee-high.
4) Practice down on your back.
5) Practice down on your sides.

Double Forearms Solo Command and Mastery

Take one or more powerful steps with each movement for power and balance.

The 12 o'clock or high double strike.

The 3 o'clock or right side double strike.

The 6 o'clock or low strike.

The 9 o'clock or left double strike.

Remember to experiment with ground strikes.

The Strikes
1) The high, or 12 o'clock strike.
2) The right side or 3 o'clock strike.
3) The low quarter or 6 o'clock strike.
4) The left side or 9 o'clock strike.

The Practice
-with free moving footwork.
-knee-high.
-down on your back.
-down on your sides.

Forearm Power Strike Developing

Strike training objects (10 strikes per set)
Hit focus mitts, sports pads, heavy bags and posts. They can be done two ways, alone and with a training partner. Like in boxing training methodologies, a trainer can flash a mitt, stalk, and evade to enliven sessions.

> 10 Thrusting right forearms
> 10 Thrusting left forearms
>
> 10 Hooking forearms to 12 o'clock
> 10 Hooking forearms to 3 o'clock
> 10 Hooking forearms to 6 o'clock
> 10 Hooking forearms to 9 o'clock
>
> 10 Double forearms to 12 o'clock
> 10 Double forearms to 3 o'clock
> 10 Double forearms to 6 o'clock
> 10 Double forearms to 9 o'clock
>
> Execute right-handed
> Execute left-handed
> Execute standing
> Execute kneeling
> Execute on your back

The Forearm Strike Statue Drill
The statue format introduced back in ***Training Mission One*** introduces to a new student, and reminds an old practitioner of thorough doctrine. The student works across the body. Outside, inside, split, inside, outside.

The statue arms can be high, low, mixed, pumping and in classic one-step, punch positions.

> Remember the statue drills can cover:
> -High fixed arms
> -Low fixed arms
> -Mixed high and low
> -Pumping arm action
> -Punching arm into a position near the prior practice zones.

These are two possibilities of fighting contact-the point where and when two bodies clash. Contact is made, either by your aggression and his block, or from your defense-blocking his aggression. Arms meet. Contact. Some systems refer to this contact point as a reference point. Either way, the statue drill really explores and explains this to new students. It prepares them for the higher level, faster training later.

Passing across a training partner from outside, inside, split, inside, outside develops a simple, comprehensive training experience. Failing to see and do this drill usually causes a practitioner to miss a contact point possibility, leaving a link missing in comprehensive doctrine.

In the series above, the first contact drives right in as a palm strike. The other hand remains up to offer cover. In the series on the next page, contact is established and the other hand charges in to strike with a forearm attack.

Same-side contact.

Opposite arm crosses over for contact.

The statue drill establishes the two main applications. The first set teaches your contact hand/arm to immediately strike. The second set teaches the other hand to immediately strike. These mechanics must be absorbed.

Forearm Strike Statue Drills: The same-side hand/arm makes contact and then strikes series.

Outside arm contact, right arm.

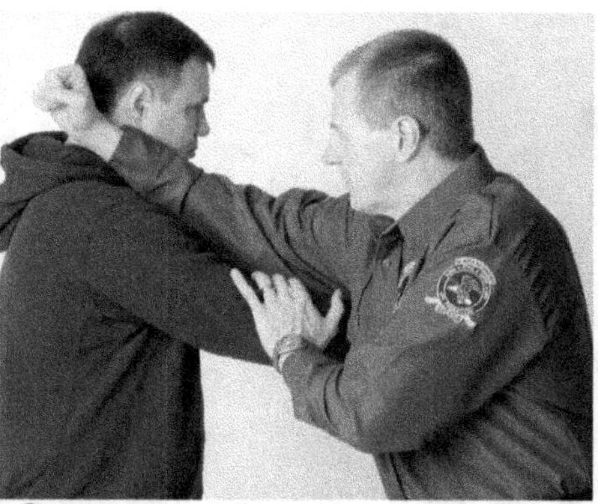
Same arm strikes. Note cover hand.

Inside arm contact, right arm.

Same arm strikes.

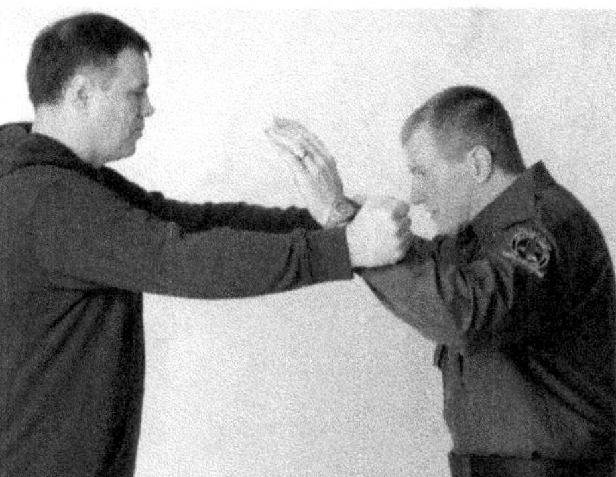
Inside split.

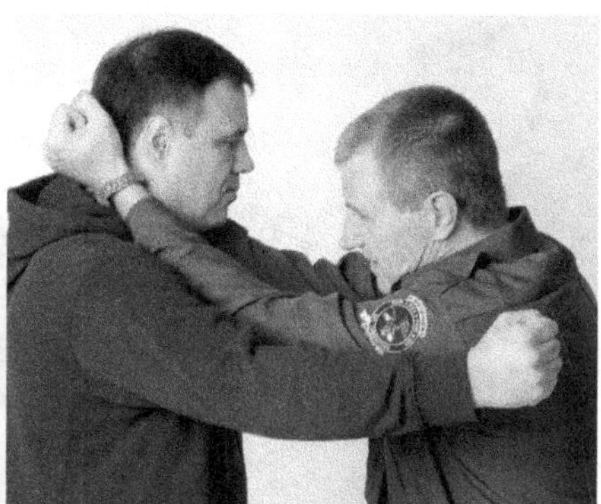
Double forearms.

Inside arm contact, left arm.

Same arm strikes.

Outside arm contact, left arm.

Statue progression

Outside arm
Inside arm
Split arm
Inside arm
Outside arm

Same arm strikes.

Forearm can strike with:

Top of the forearm
Bottom of the forearm
Back of the forearm
Inside of the forearm

Outside arm contact.

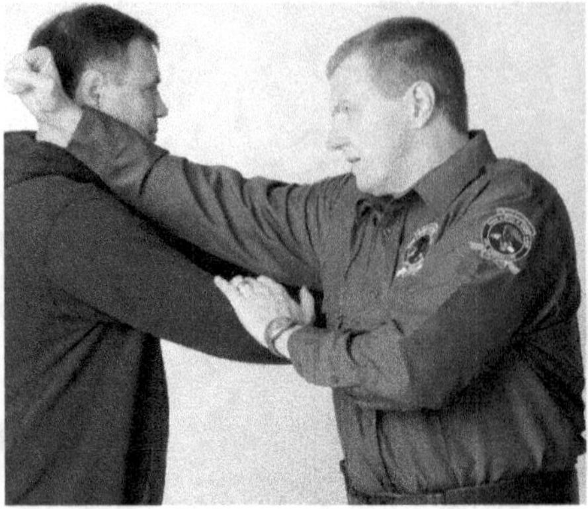

Free arm strikes.

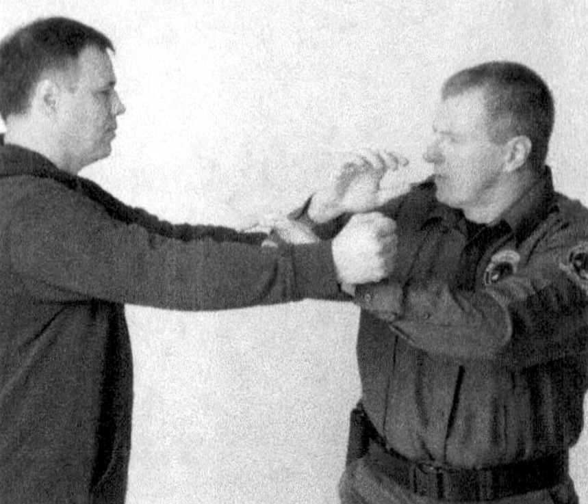

Inside arm contact.

Free arm strikes.

Double arm split contact.

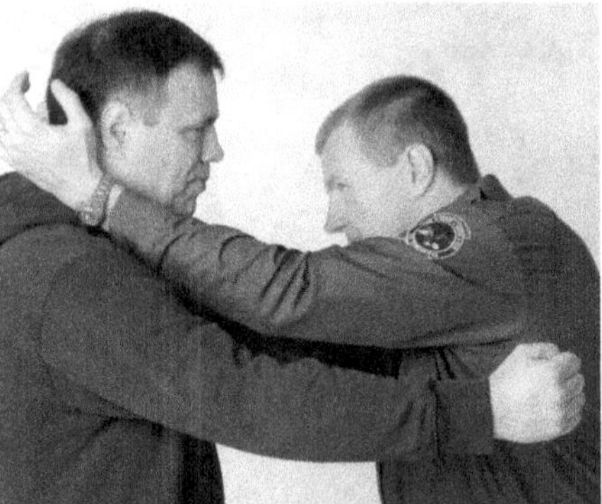

Double arm strike.

Inside arm contact.

Free arm strikes.

Outside arm contact.

The throat doesn't have to be the only target. You can also strike other targets.

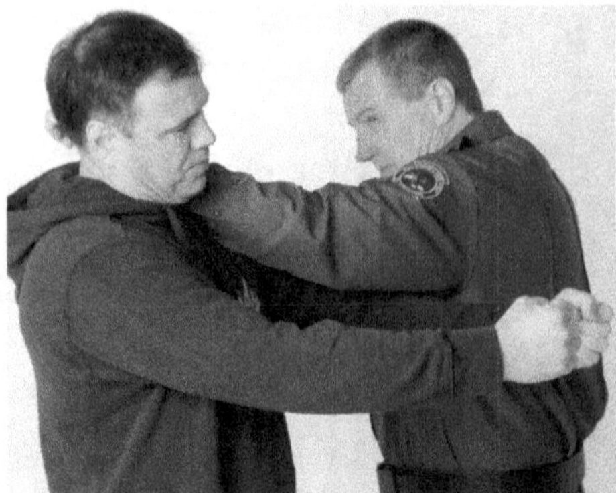

Free arm strikes.

Other targets may be:

The face
The neck (as shown)
The arms
The torso
The groin

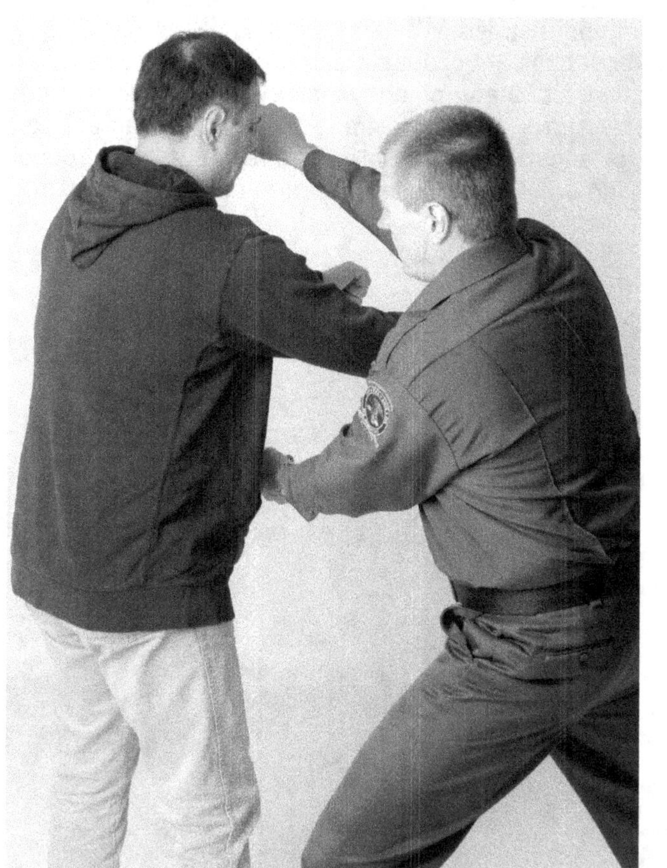 

Work the statue drill to also exercise the double arm strikes.

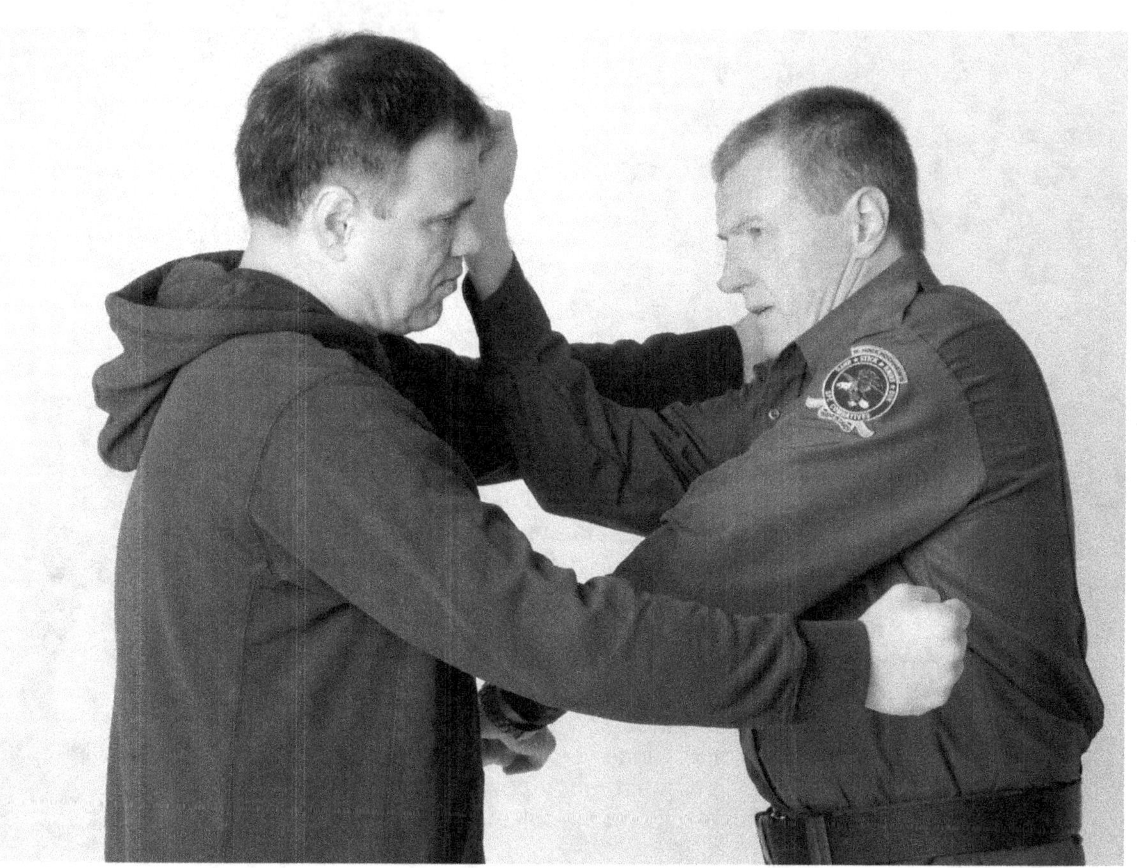

The Forearm Blocks

Some people just love techno jargon and acronyms. They wax philosophical for hours on the nerve endings and psycho babble that cause us to do this, that or the other movement under stress. Way less talk and much more walk still explains it all and gets the job done. I love this photo of a slipped baseball bat because it demonstrates the two very common responses used when under sudden attack. Note the positions of the arms and since everyone is seated, the raising of the knee. Even standing people will often raise a leg under attack, all in a desire to protect the head and torso.

Here in ***Training Mission Three,*** the subject of forearm as a tool is introduced officially. As a result of this introduction, it is only fitting that an overview of unarmed combatives blocking be presented, as a forearm usually is an instrumental part of many blocks.

These two universal blocks, two of several, are the ***Two Arm Block,*** shown to the left and the ***Zone Block***, on the right. Both are executed in the 9 o'clock positions.

Both are just as easily executed as the other, both as reflexive. And, it is easy to see that the Zone Block covers much more space and if this photo is any evidence, this block just happens naturally.

There is no perfect block, just the right one for the moment. Key to how you block will be the position of your hands and arms the second before the attack. Since you will be attacked from ambushes and combat ready positions, it is wise to practice all blocks on the following pages.

Two Arm Block

Zone Block

UC Block 1: The Unsupported Block

3 o'clock   6 o'clock   9 o'clock   12 o'clock

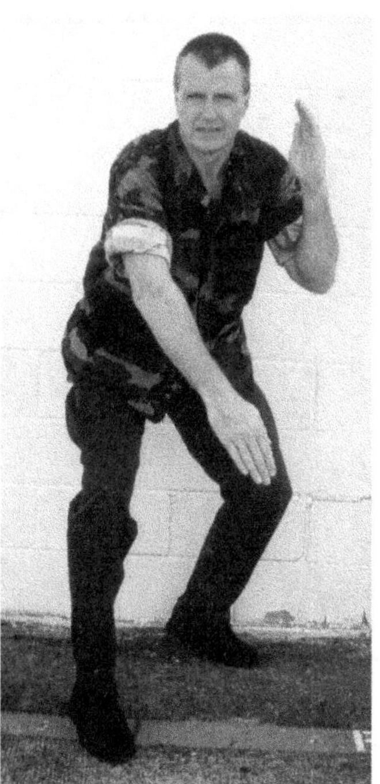

Sweep under the clock, for all that low-line junk that might invade in.

   This is a single arm block. Remember the proper, total body synergy to energize the block. Use from the tip of the elbow on up to the tightened fingers of your hand. Use your torso and legs to mobilize the effort. Simply think of playing football, basketball, rugby or soccer to inspire your movement.

UC Block 2: Single Arm versus a Knife Attack

When faced with a knife attack, all experts agree that a block should have a bladed or turned forearm in such a manner that the delicate muscles and blood vessels are inside and away from the edge of the knife. Take this course of action even if you have several layers of clothing on. Clothing helps, but is no cure. You will see this advice again and again in our Knife/Counter-Knife course.

3 o'clock   6 o'clock   9 o'clock   12 o'clock

Steve Krsytek sweeps under the clock against a low line knife attack.

"There is no perfect block, just the right one for the moment. The key to how you block will be the position of your hands and arms the second before the attack. Since you will be attacked from ambushes and combat ready positions, it is wise to practice all blocks on these pages."

UC Block 3: The Two-Arm Block

| 3 o'clock | 6 o'clock | 9 o'clock | 12 o'clock |

The elbows of the arms can be canted in different angles to help the block.

UC Block 4: The Zone Block

| 3 o'clock | 6 o'clock | 9 o'clock | 12 o'clock |

Zone blocking is a term commonly used in western boxing, where it usually originates from a standard dukes up boxing pose. The boxer turns to avoid a punch, and the arms just fall into these positions. This bent-arm block, one half of the zone movement, is found in many established martial systems.

UC Block 5: The Supported Block

3 o'clock

6 o'clock

9 o'clock

12 o'clock

In my studies of Indonesian and Thailand fighting systems, I have come across the supported block. At a moment of impact, perceived to be severe, the other arm comes in to help. Think of this as having to push open really heavy double doors. The move also sets up Indo and Thai crashes into the opponent's body and blurs the line between defense and offense.

UC Block 6: The Torso Crunch

The arm covers the torso.

UC Block 7: The Shoulder Crunch

The shoulder rises. The chin drops.

UC Block 8: The Doomsday Block

UC Block 9: The Fist Breaker Block

Usually reserved for last ditch, ground fighting protection.

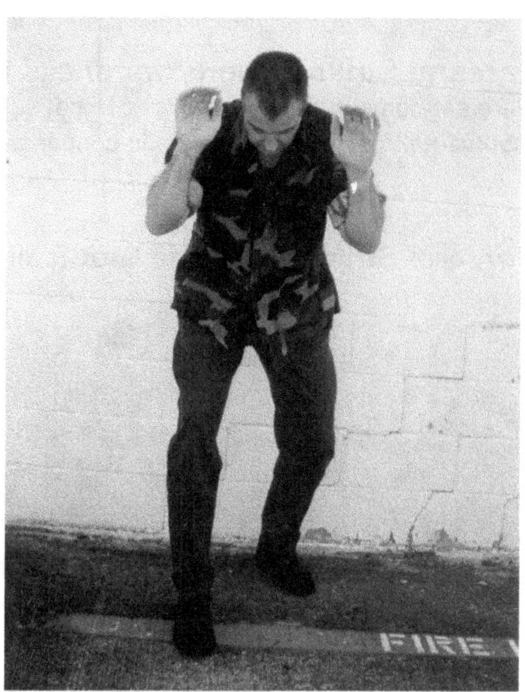

An old dock fighting and bare knuckle fighter trick. Last ditch effort. Lower your skull and hope the attacker breaks his hand.

UC Block 10: All Strikes Can be Blocks too!

Some systems like to say, "We never block. We always strike. But really that is just a question of semantics. Sometimes, everyone simply and reflexively blocks. But where and when possible, always hurt the enemy with a block. And to continue, practice a strike after each block. Counter attack!

Counter Attack!

Forearm Strike Option Awareness Combat Scenarios

Here are some option awareness combat scenarios you can practice that involve forearm strikes. Keep in mind that the palm strike can be used in countless ways, inside countless scenarios.

Forearm Strike CS 1: The Clothesline

Looks like the fight is on!

The strike is blocked.

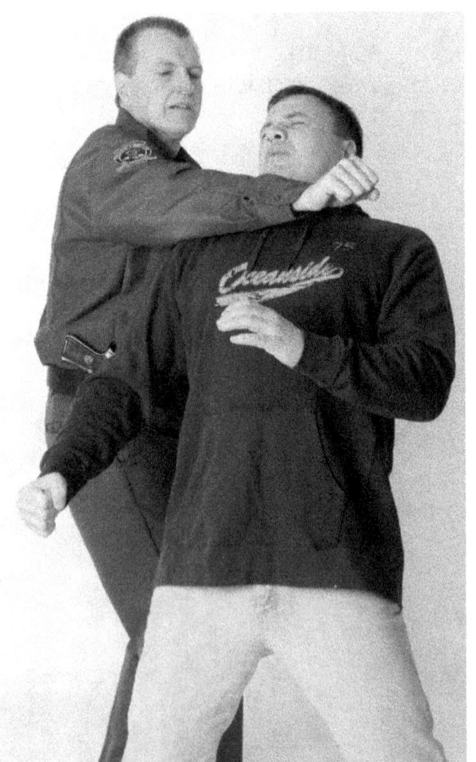

The opponent is clotheslined. The forearm must hit and turn downward.

The Forearm Strike Block, Pass and Pin Drill

As with **Training Mission One** and **Two,** we will use the six-count block, pass and pin drill to develop skill and savvy. Feel the flow of action and feel of energy. See our Training Mission DVDs to really capture the motion. The basic steps are:

1) He strikes. You block.

2) He is passed with your forearm.

3) He is pinned with your limb.

4) He counters your forearm strike.

5) He passes your strike.

6) He pins you.

Above are the basic six steps. In this particular forearm strike drill, we ask that students concentrate on using their forearms since that is subject of this module. Lead with a palm strike and try to use your palms for all manipulations. Most practitioners practice the high right attack version. In the complete program, there are four corners of palm attacks for this drill- high right attack, high left attack, low right attack and low left attack.

> BPP Drill Corner 1) -high right forearm downward strike to start.
> BPP Drill Corner 2) -high left forearm downward strike to start.
> BPP Drill Corner 3) -low uppercut forearm up from the right to start.
> BPP Drill Corner 4) -low uppercut forearm up from the left to start.
>
> Do the above walking back and forth and sideways. Then change the range.
> Do them on the ground, on your back versus someone kneeling and then side-to-side.

Performing these drills is not mandatory for performance testing, they are great skill developers. Never overdo skill drills at the expense of other training. Always have a drill or two for the development of each tactic. This block, pass and pin drill always brings tremendous coordination and speed.

Forearm Strike 1/2 Beat insert practice

As a veteran of **Training Mission One,** you should already understand the mechanics of this drill and its half beat inserts. In this application, we look at two general skill goals.

> Goal 1) Develop Quick Counter Attacks
> Goal 2) Develop unique movements and applications

The next series of photos will document some 1/2 beat strikes. They will fall after the main beats. The first series utilizes the blocking contact hand as an immediate follow-up striker.

The next series of photos will document some 1/2 beat strikes. They will fall after the main beats. The first series utilizes the blocking contact hand as an immediate follow-up striker.

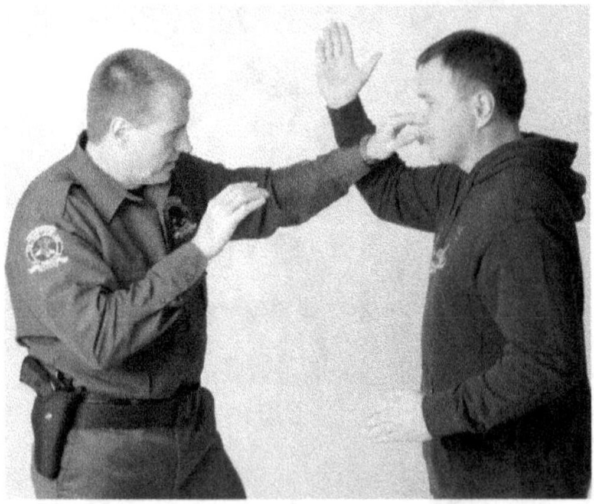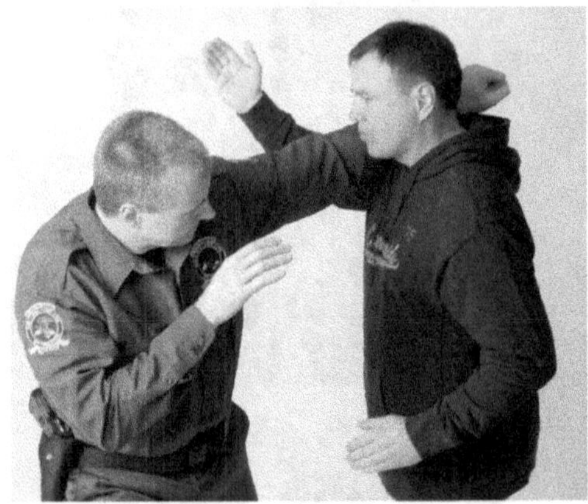

Insert Basic 1) Beat 1 1/2 contact and same arm strikes.

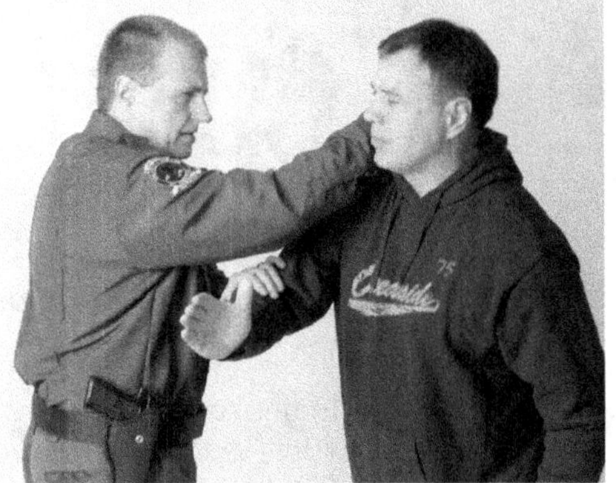

Beat 2 1/2 contact and strike. The attacking arm rakes across the enemy's arm to the target.

Beat 3 1/2 contact and same arm strike. Note the constant arm-to-arm contact.

Work these both right hand and left handed, high and low corners. Become a fighting expert, not a drill expert. These drills exist purely for coordination and insert development.

Insert Basic Series 2) The other hand immediately forearm strikes.
Execute it as quickly as possible, ergo the phrase Beat 1-to-1 and 1/2. Simultaneous block and strike contacts would be desirable.

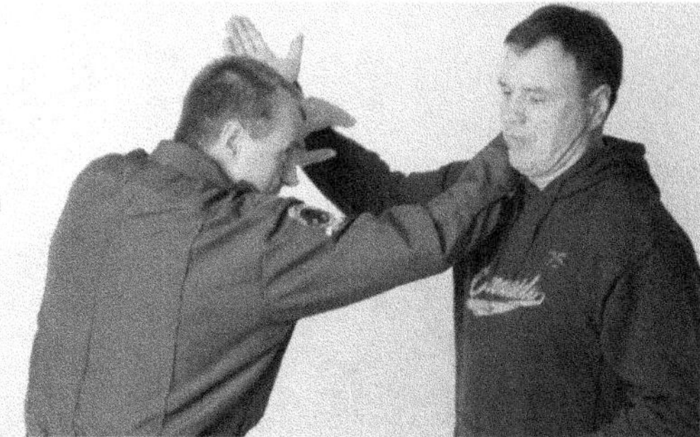

Beat 1 and 1 1/2 The free arm strikes.

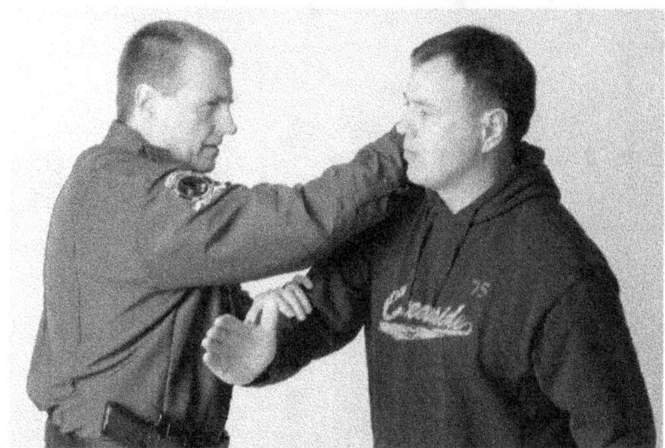

Beat 2 to 2 1/2 The other arm strikes as quickly as possible

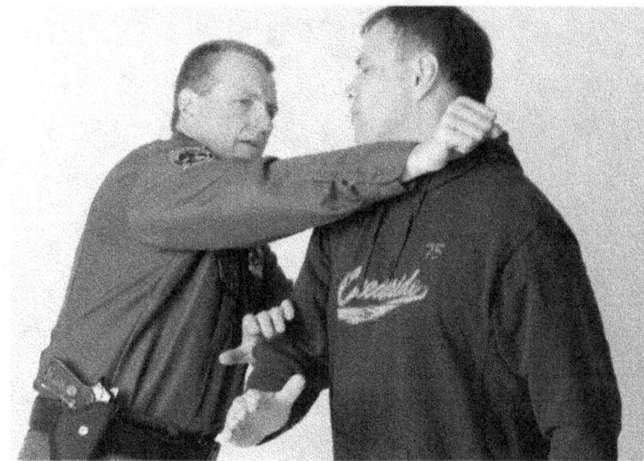

Beat 3 to 3 1/2. The other hand strikes as quickly as possible.

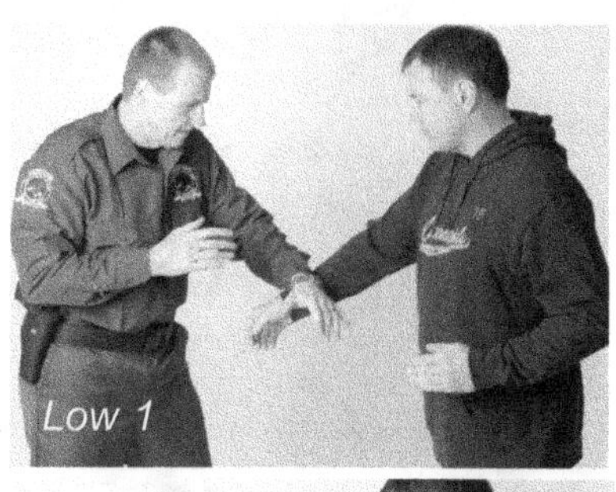

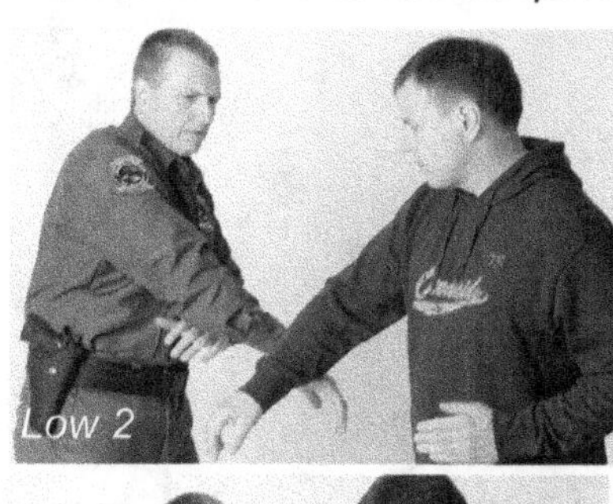

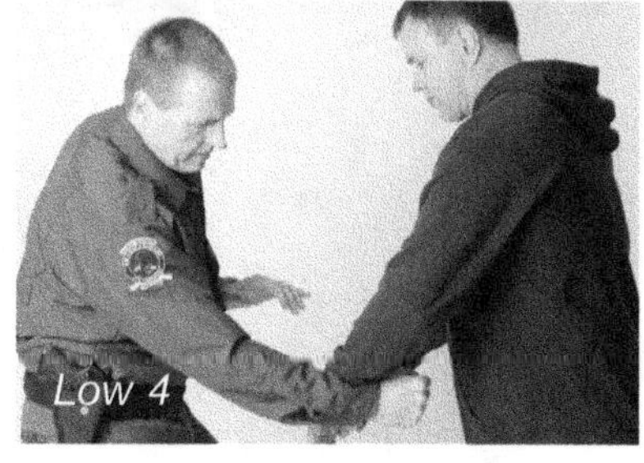

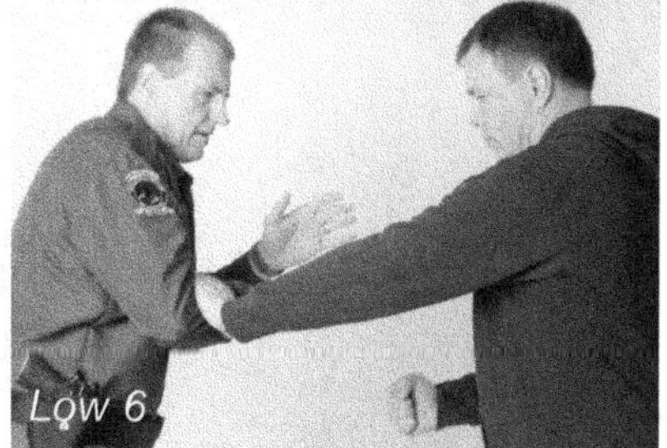

Forearm Strike CS 2: The Groin Strike
Again we fight against the common angry choke or any extended arm grab around the collar or shoulder.

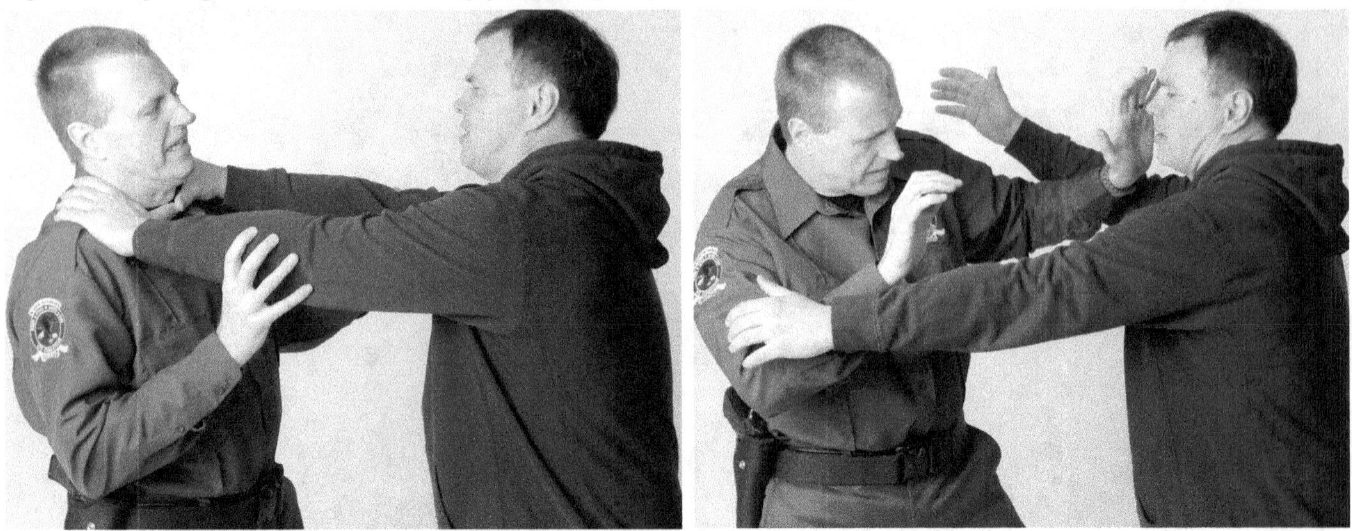

A common choke attack is broken apart. An eye is attacked in the process.

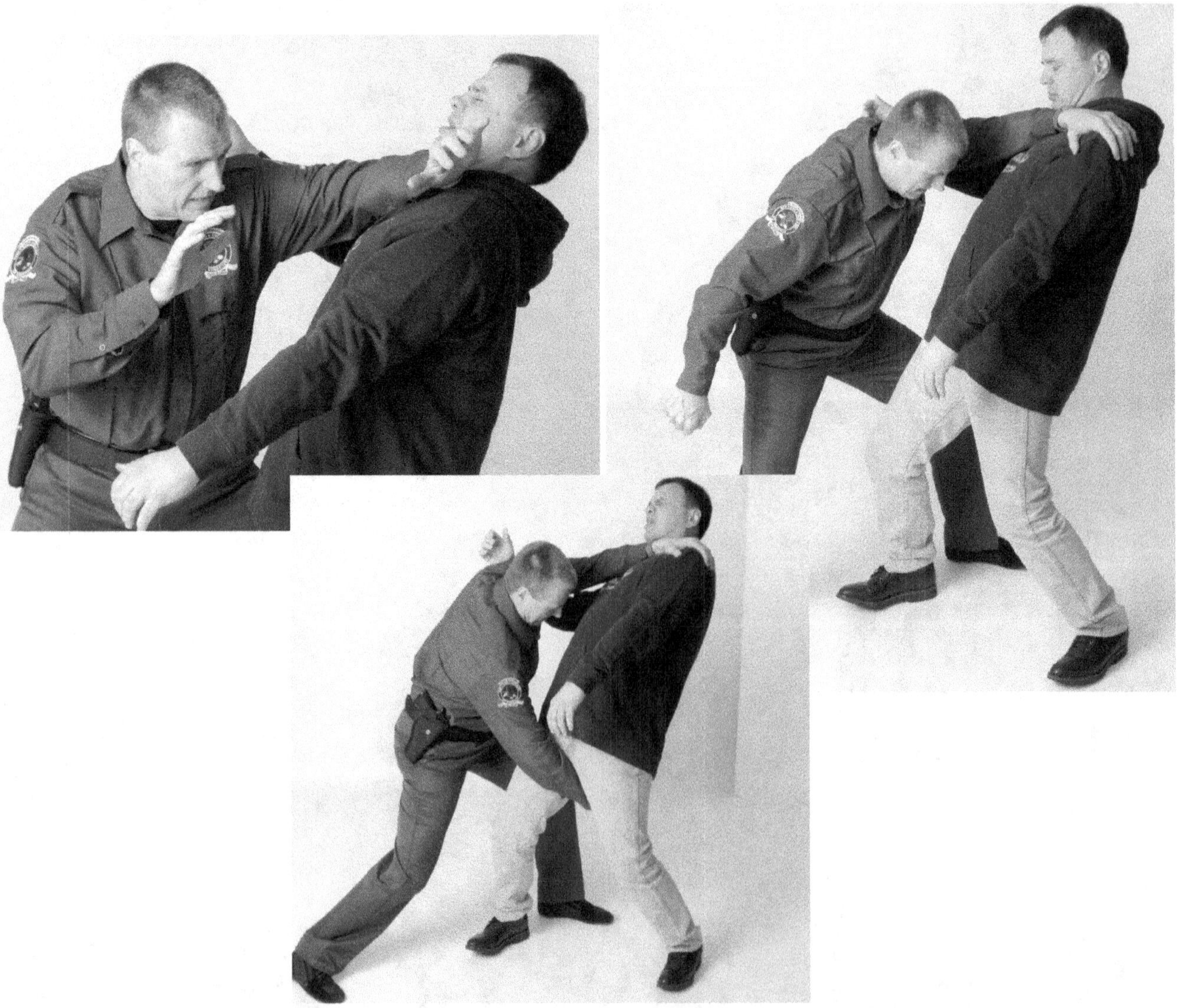

Unarmed Combatives
Level 3 Kick: The Knee Strike

The knee strike is a powerful close quarter leg attack.

Knee Strike Studies and Observations 1) Targeting

The main targets of the knee are the groin, thighs, and possibly the lower stomach and torso area, when the enemy is standing upright. If the enemy is bent over, even his head can drop into range. Once grounded, knee strikes can land anywhere.

Versus a standing enemy:
        Target 1) The groin
        Target 2) The circumference of the thigh.
        Target 3) Any targets, if the enemy is bent over.
        Target 4) Knee drops to any targets if the enemy is downed.

Knee to groin.

Knee to the thigh.

Knee to bent-over body.

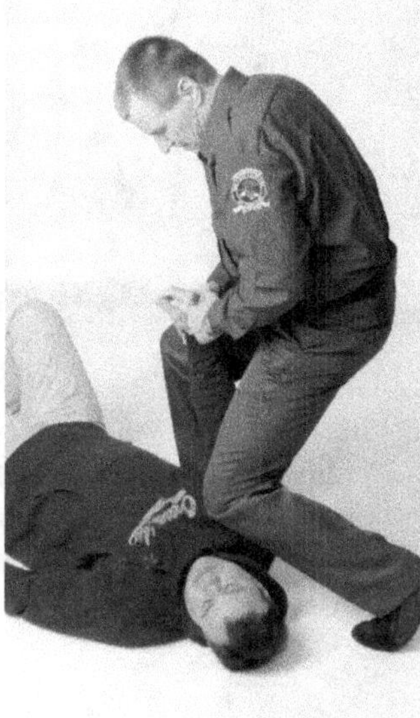

Knee to prone targets.

Ground Power Knee

Versus a prone enemy:
    Prone targets 1) The whole prone body, face up or down.
    Prone targets 2) Smaller points like hands. The target depends on your circumstance.

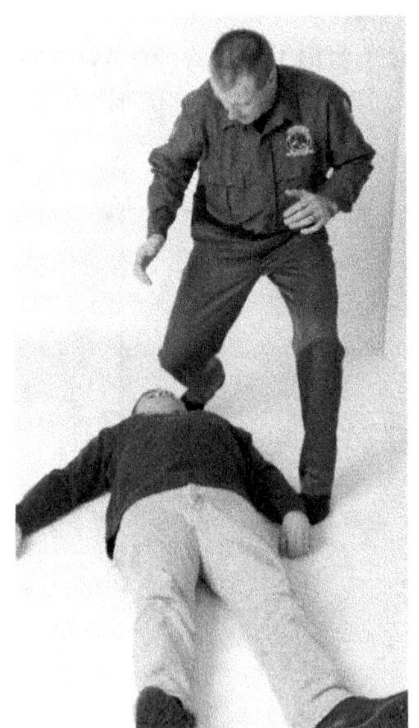
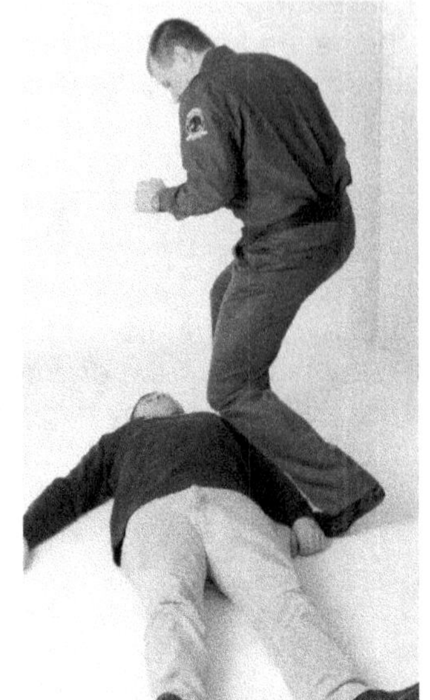

Knees to grounded face, neck, ankle, knee, ribs and hands.

Knee Strike Skill and Flow Developing Drills

Knee Drill 1) The Outside/Inside Knee Strike Drill

There are two versions of this drill, one where the training partners face each other, and one where the trainer holds the trainee in a bear hug. In both positions, the trainee builds stomp kick muscle memory through repetition and is a must for a new student to practice these options. Throughout the practice, the trainer stands in place so that the trainee can develop basic skills. The trainee makes several passes across the body.

1) Outside knee strike.   *2) Front leg strike.*   *3) Inner leg strike.*   *4 & 5) R & L groin strikes.*

6) Inside left leg strike.

7) Front leg strike.

8) Outside leg strike.

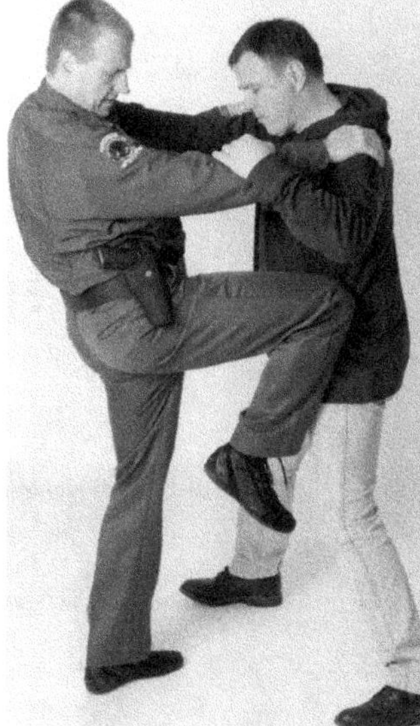

9) Side knee to rib.

10) Hooking knee to torso.

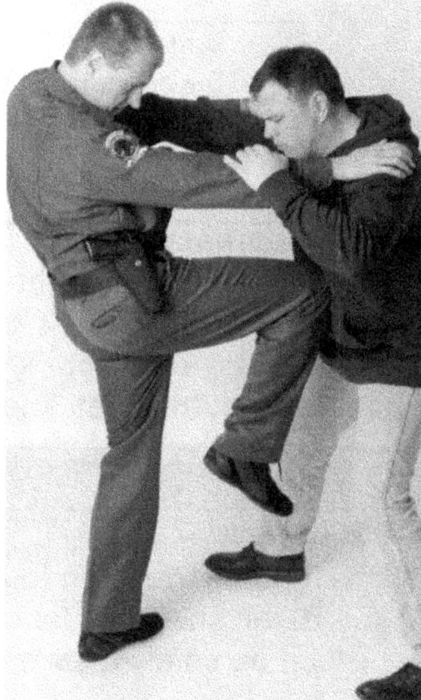

11) Right thrust to torso.

12) Left thrust to torso.

13) Hooking knee to torso.

14) Left side-knee.

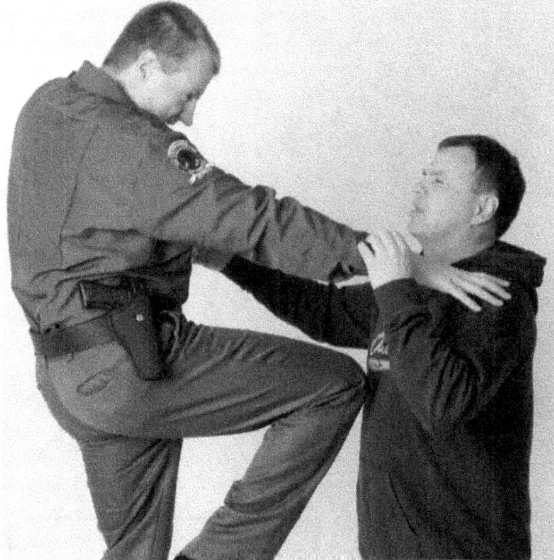

15 and 16) R. and L. Leaping thrust knees.

The Knee Drill:
1) Left knee to outside right leg
2) Best knee to right leg front
3) Left knee to inside right leg
4) Left knee to groin
5) Right knee to groin
6) Left knee to inside left leg
7) Best knee to left leg front
8) Right knee to outside left leg
9) Right side knee to torso
10) Right hooking knee to torso
11) Right thrust knee to torso
12) Left thrust knee to torso
13) Left hooking knee to torso
14) Left side knee to torso
15) Leaping left knee to torso
16) Leaping right knee to torso

Knee Drill 2) Power Practice with Pads and Devices

We need to develop power and target acquisition skill for the knee from standing and practical ground positions.

-10 standing knee strikes with the right leg.
-10 standing knee strikes with the left leg.

-10 knee drops with the right leg.
-10 knee drops with the left leg.

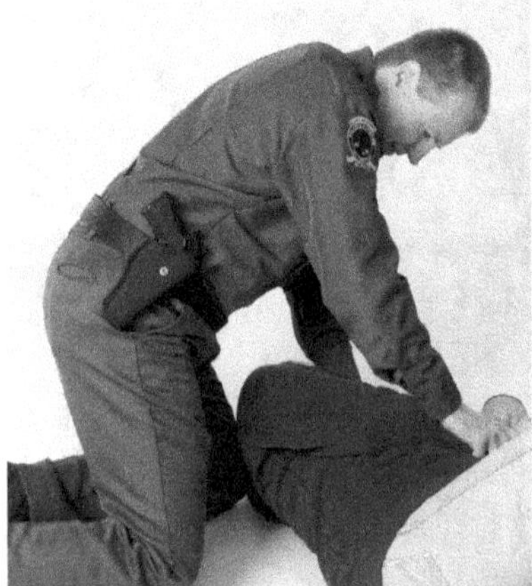

Standing Combinations
-10 sets, double right knees.
-10 sets, double left knees.
-10 sets, triple right knees.
-10 sets, triple left knees.

Ground Knees
-10 right knees on four quarters.
-10 left knees on four quarters.
*Get up safely after each set of 10.

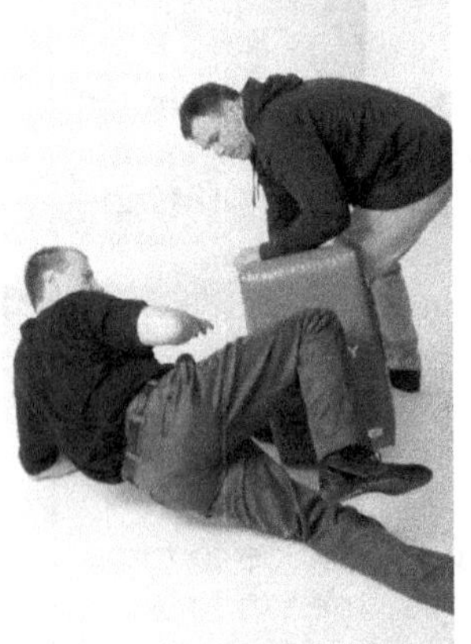

-10 rollover right knees.
-10 rollover left knees.
*Get up after each set.

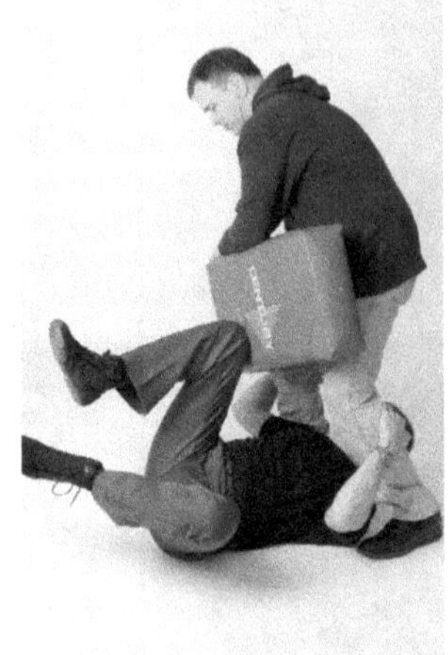

-10 right knees up.

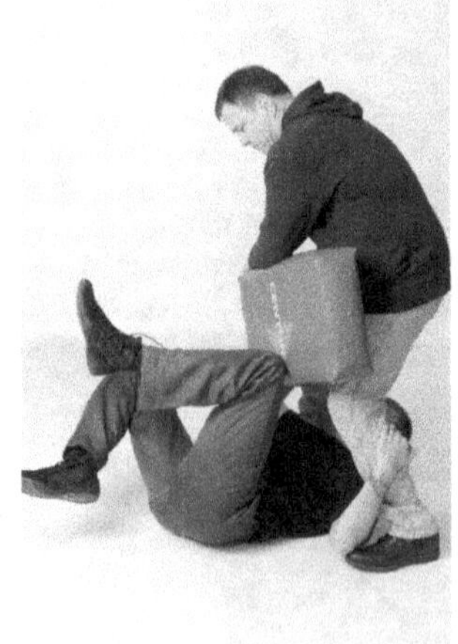

-10 left knees up.

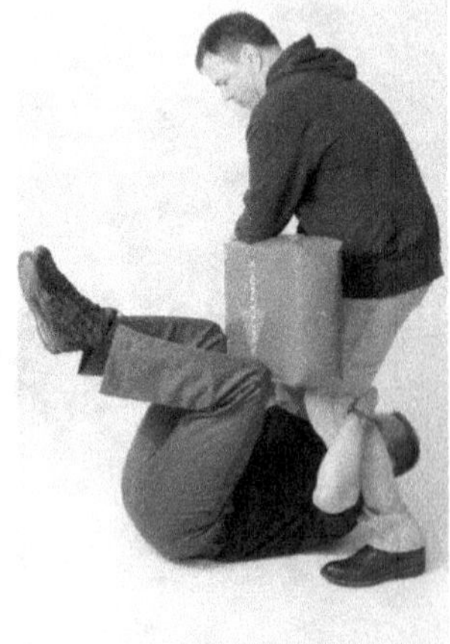

-10 double knees up.

Knee Strike Option Awareness Combat Scenarios (OACS) Knee versus Puncher

After performing some of the skill drills, the knee strike applications should be obvious. Here are a few samples, two of which are not often seen demonstrated, but are often quite viable.

Knee OACS 1) Block, Knee, Hammer Down

The opponent shoves you or punches you. You block, forearm strike, then try to grab the arm and pull the stunned man down. Deliver any angle of knee attack you need to hit the torso. Jump, if need be. Batter him down.

1) Counter and eye attack.

2) Forearm crash to neck.

3) Pull down and knee.

4) Batter the opponent down. Apply strikes as needed.

Knee Strike Option Awareness Combat Scenarios: Knee versus Knifer Cross-Draw

  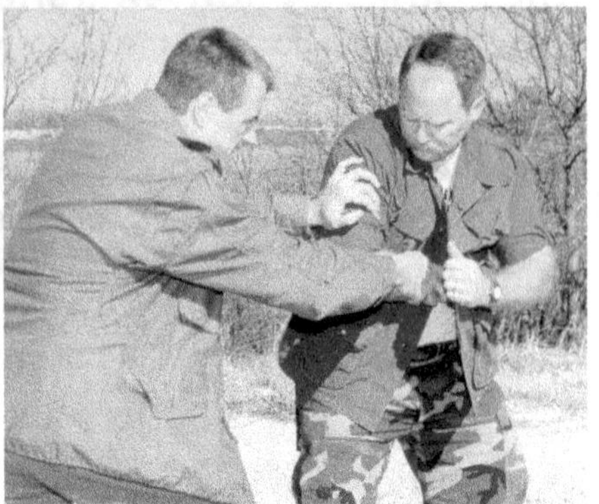

You spot the hand traveling into a weapon cross-draw. You react immediately with a charge.

The classic knee strike.

The knife is still coming out! The arm wrap.

Rear arm bar.

Knee strike to leg buckle.

Drive him down.

Get the knife.

UC Takedowns 4: The Rear Takedowns Module

This basic collection records the common rear takedowns, when you force your opponent straight down over his heels and onto his back.

RT 1) The Leg Sweep/Reap:
Outer Leg Studies and Observations 1) The one-leg or two-leg sweeps are practiced by many. Sometimes it is difficult for your leg to reach across the enemy's spread legs. Get the lower body moving forward.

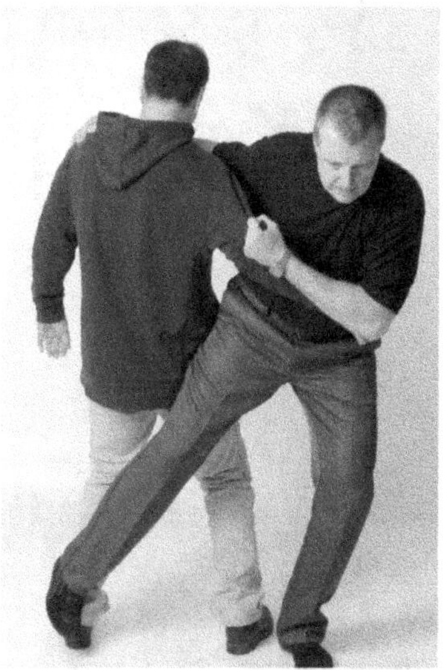
Two-leg outer sweep/reap.

One-leg outer sweep/reap.

Avoid the small target of heel kick to calf.

Outer Leg Studies and Observations 1) Get the upper body moving back. Strike and push upon:
   Strike/Push 1: Chin
   Strike/Push 2: Eye strike and push over and down.
   Strike/Push 3: Clavicle smash.
   Strike/Push 4: Elbow smash/compression.

Chin

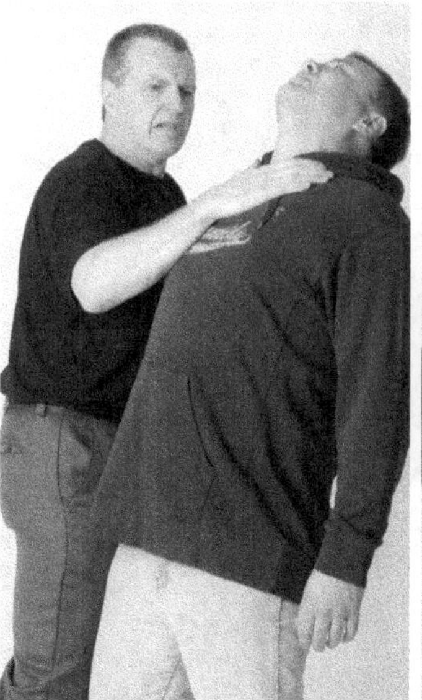
Over and down eye push

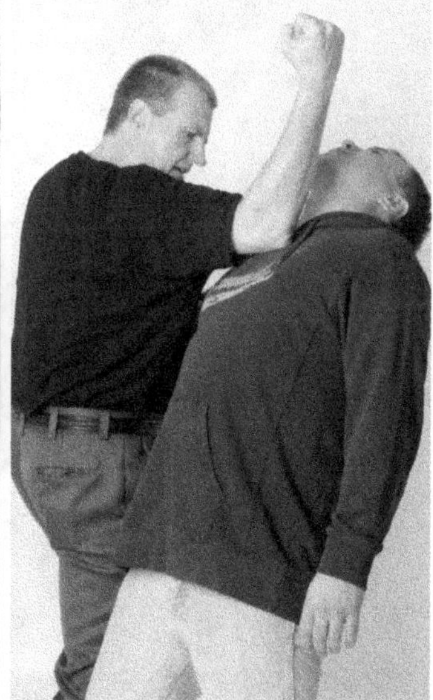
Clavicle smash

Elbow

Military Head Bash Version

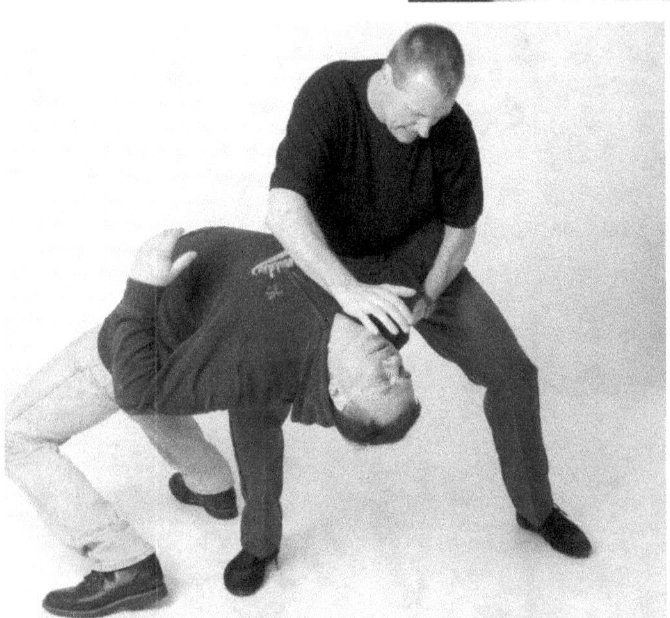

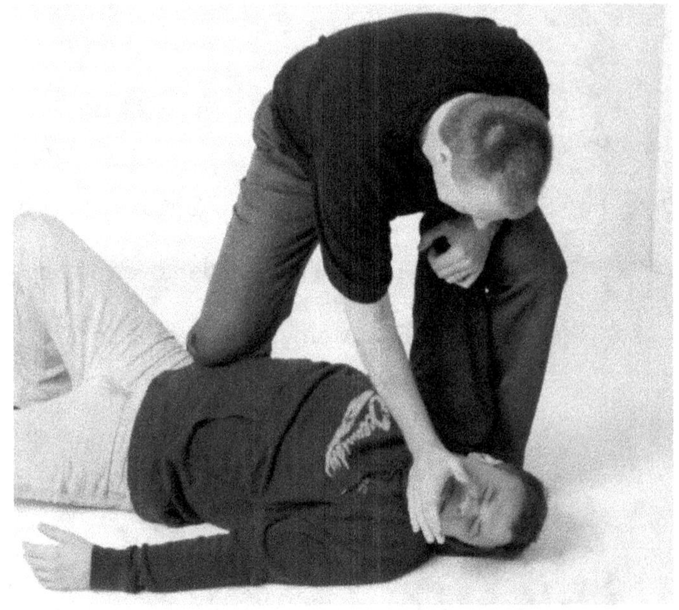

Avoid just curling the leg.

Bending forward helps.

Avoid just barely curling your leg around an enemy. You might fight to get into that close position, but if you stop advancing and simply, barely, wrap your leg around his leg, you are in a side-by-side position and have lost your momentum. He now also has YOU in a leg curl too! Strongest man wins! Drive past an imaginary line of his heels, pulling the arm, as the second photo above shows. Then kick back. Bending forward in your charge helps.

Counters to the Rear Leg Sweep Takedown

Turn into the person.

Step your inner leg back.

Double the force. Increase the momentum so you can roll to a topside position.

RT 2: Inner Leg Reap: Should the outer leg be unaccessible to your quick reap? Troubleshoot by reaping a leg from the inside as one possibility. Assist with a knee strike to the inner thigh or knee.

Charge in.

Inner leg knee strike.

Back kick behind the knee...

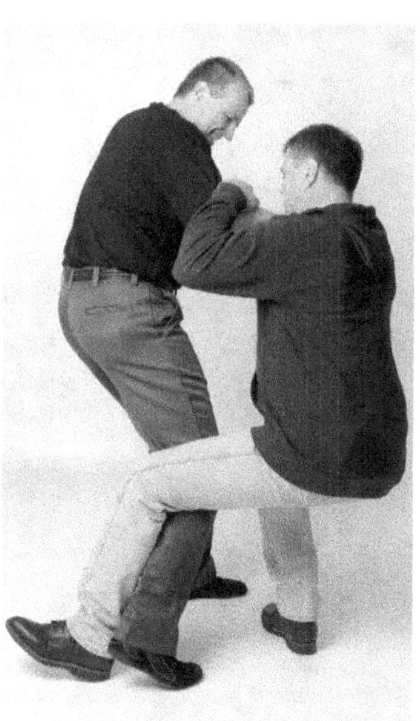

...you push him back and down.

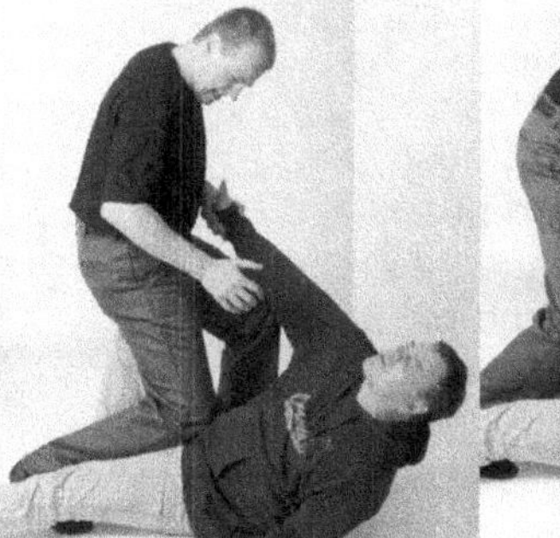

Finish with a knee to the groin and a knee to the face.

The Leg Sweep/Reap Statute Drill

  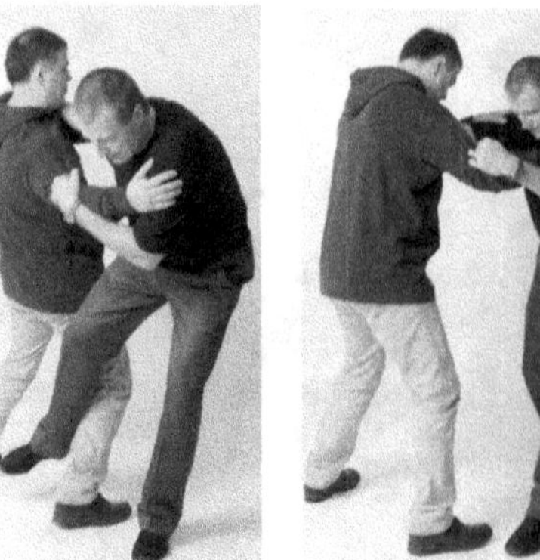  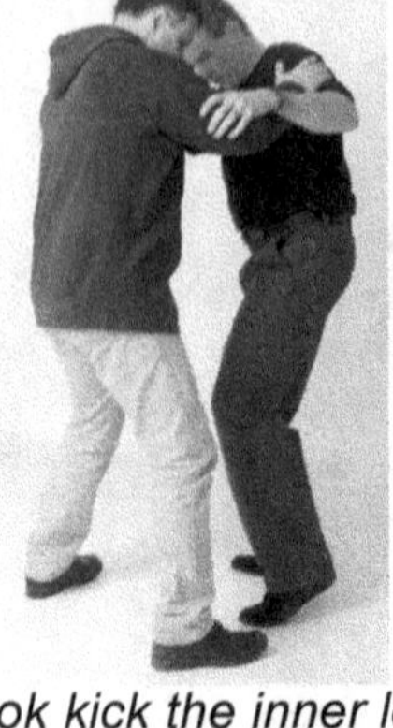

Neutral start.   *Step out, hook, reap and pull.*   *Step in, back hook kick the inner leg and push.*

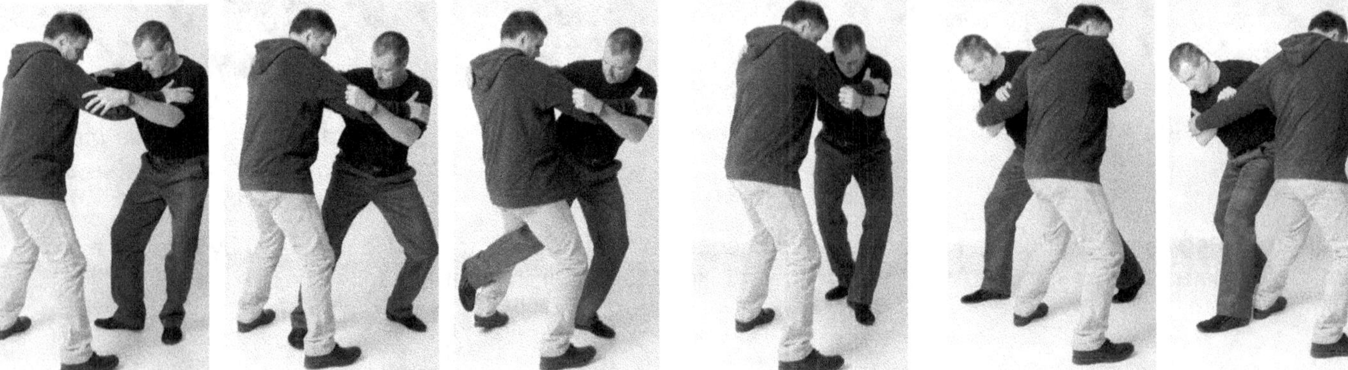

Step in, back hook kick the inner leg and push.   *Step out, hook, reap and pull.*

This version of the statue drill helps introduce and package the leg reaps/sweeps that cause an opponent to fall backward. Push on the upper torso and pull on the seized arm just enough to feel the initiation of the takedown. Then, move on to the next step. On the inner leg reaps you may practice the set-up knee strike previously shown.

The Basic Progression:

1) Neutral position.
2) Hook the outer left leg and push.
3) Hook the inner left leg and push.
4) Hook the inner right leg and push.
5) Hook the outer right leg and push.

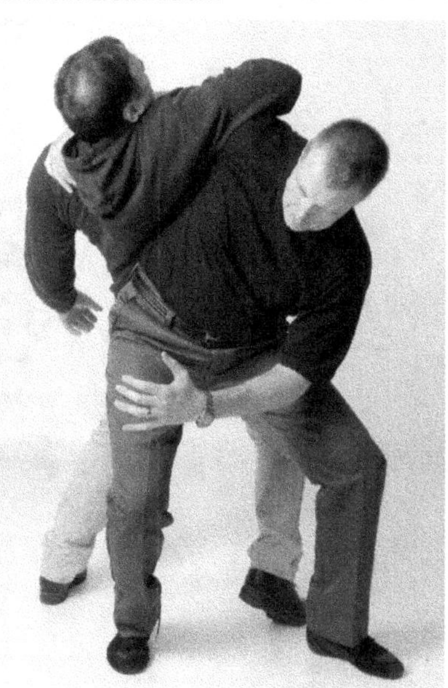 

I teach the Reverse Hip Throw as an extension of the Rear leg takedown, when the enemy counters your attempt at a rear leg sweep. Stun severely first. Should the opponent step with his inside leg way forward as you charge in, an option is to slip you hip deep behind his, the small of your back to the small of his back. Step deeply as needed. Then you lower your belt line as low as possible by bending at your knees. Cant a hip for maximum effect. Rip him over the top.

Stun first.
Should the opponent step with his inside leg way forward as you charge in.
Slip your hip deep behind his, the small of your back to the small of his back.
Lower your belt line as low as possible by bending at your knees.
Cant a hip for maximum effect. Rip him over the top.

RT 4) The Rear Pull Takedown

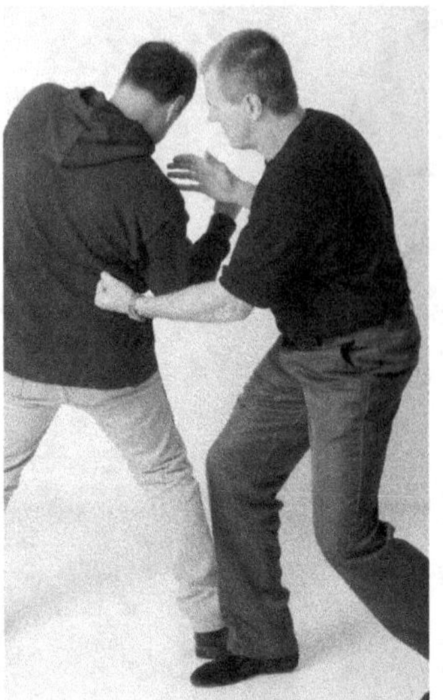

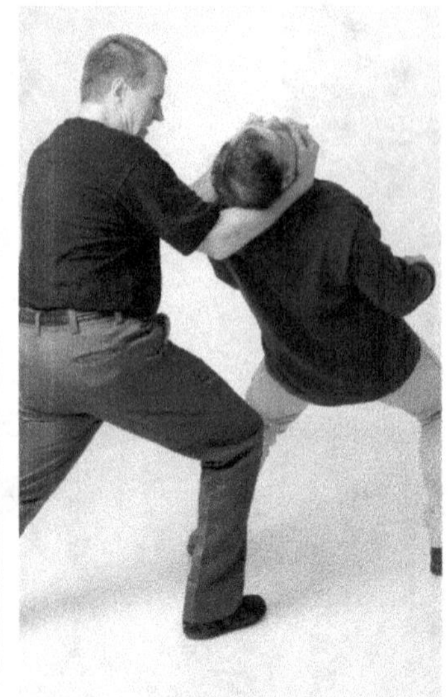

Get behind the attacker. *Cup your hands on the chin. Tip the chin up. Pull down.*

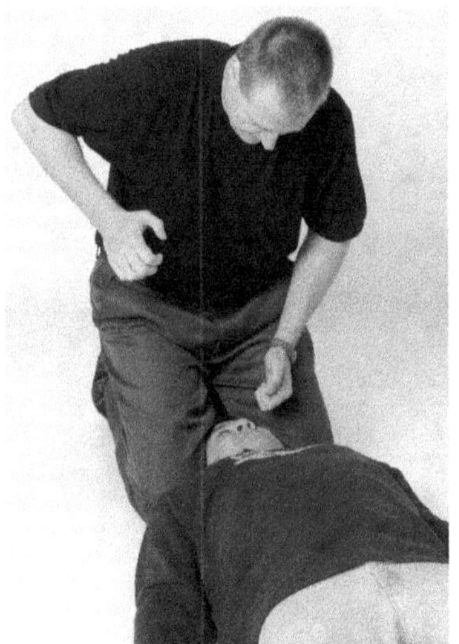

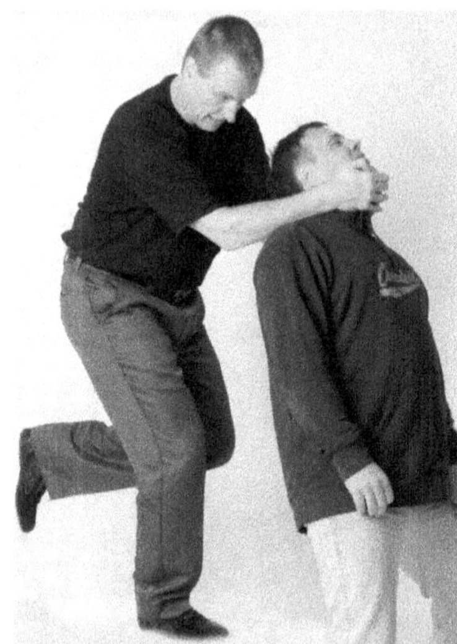

Attack! *Variations: Pull the belt line.* *Leap in the air and pull down.*

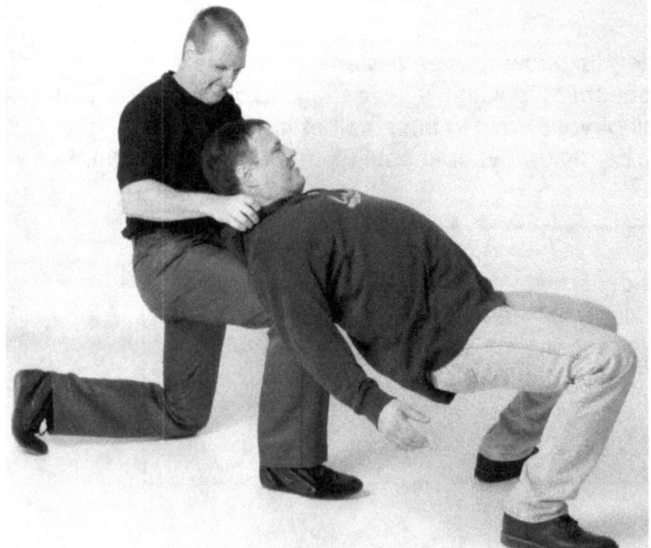
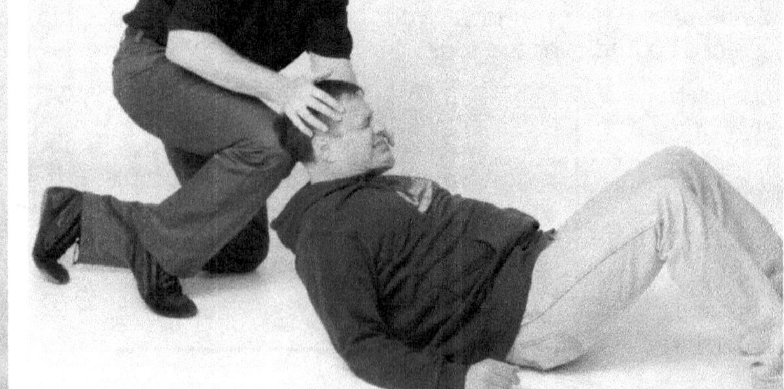

Variations: Pull the attacker's back down on your knee, or his head down on your knee.

Your Level 3 Unarmed Combatives Summary and Workout

Practice...

___ Thrusting Forearms
- -10 right arm.
- -10 left arm.

___ Hooking Forearms
- -10 single arm from each corner right arm.
- -10 single arm from each clock corner left arm.
- -10 double arms from each clock corner.

___ Knee strikes
- -10 right standing
- -10 left standing
- -10 right knee drops
- -10 left knee drops
- -10 sets double right
- -10 sets double left
- -10 sets triple right
- -10 sets triple left

- -10 right roll overs
- -10 left roll-overs
- -10 right up overs on back
- -10 left up overs left on back
- -10 right and left up overs on back

___ Any 6 Combat Scenarios using Rear Takedowns
- -2 rear sweeps
- -2 rear pulls
- -1 reverse hip throw
- -1 inner leg reap

SDMS Impact Weapon Combatives
Stick Level 3: The DMS "Dos Manos" Combat Module

In *Training Mission One* we learned how to quick draw and present the impact weapon under combat stress, whether that weapon is a long flashlight, solid stick, or expandable baton. In *Training Mission Two* we began to use the weapon in combat with a single-handed grip. Here, *Training Mission Three* introduces the two-handed stick grip.

DMS Studies and Observations 1) Review of *Training Mission One and Two:* Vital essentials about stick combatives are documented in *Training Mission One* and *Training Mission Two.* Review those before proceeding with the this segment of training.

The Protocols for DMS Combatives: Practitioners must learn striking, blocking and grappling in standing, kneeling and ground positions.

Protocol 1)	Learn the DMS strikes.
Protocol 2)	Learn the DMS blocks.
Protocol 3)	Learn the counters to common strikes.
Protocol 4)	Learn the counters to common blocks.
Protocol 5)	Incorporate SMS with DMS.

DMS Studies and Observations 2) Review the Three Basic DMS Grips

DMS Stick grip-palms down.

DMS Rifle grip-one palm up.
One palm down.

DMS Bat or sword grip.

DMS Grip 1) The "Stick Grip," with two palms down.
DMS Grip 2) The "Rifle Grip," with one palm up, one palm down.
DMS Grip 3) The "Bat Grip," with a grip as in holding a baseball bat or sword.

Studies and Observations 3) The DMS Impact Strikes

Strikes should be conservative in their delivery, yet as powerful as possible. Do not retract too far to deliver, or over-swing if you miss your target. Hit training objects as hard as possible to experience real impact shock. The impact weapon strikes with the shaft, the tip and the handle. A swing with too much shoulder movement allows an enemy to counter attack when the weapon is brought far back or when it is over done. The rearing back, or "chambering" of the stick is not a sound tactical strategy.

When you grasp the weapon with two hands there are 27 general ways to strike. They are broken down here in four easily grouped sets. The sets cover all the military, police and martial arts applications.

Group 1) DMS 15

Group 2) Surround Riot 4

Group 3) Heaven and Hell 4

Group 4) The Batting 4

Group 1) DMS 15
This collection contains the basic pommel and shaft strikes.

Group 2) Surround Riot 4
This collection centers on thrusting attacks to your front, back sides and rear.

Group 3) Heaven and Hell 4
This set of 4 covers attacks high and low.

Group 4) Batting 4
This collection covers the 4 two-handed strikes.

Practice the DMS 15 and the Heaven and Hell 4 while knee-high and on your back.

The DMS 15 Strikes

An impact weapon hits the shaft, the tip and the handle, or pommel as striking surfaces. This will be dissected in the photos and explanations that follow. As a matter of thorough training doctrine, these should be practiced standing, kneeling and on the ground. Note how rifle and/or bayonet and butt strokes apply. Remember that 10 percent of your practitioners will be lefty and will hold their long guns differently than the right-handed. Therefore a bayonet slash to a right-handed man is a bayonet slash to a lefty. I expect you to train each strike. Eventually and incidentally you will remember them.

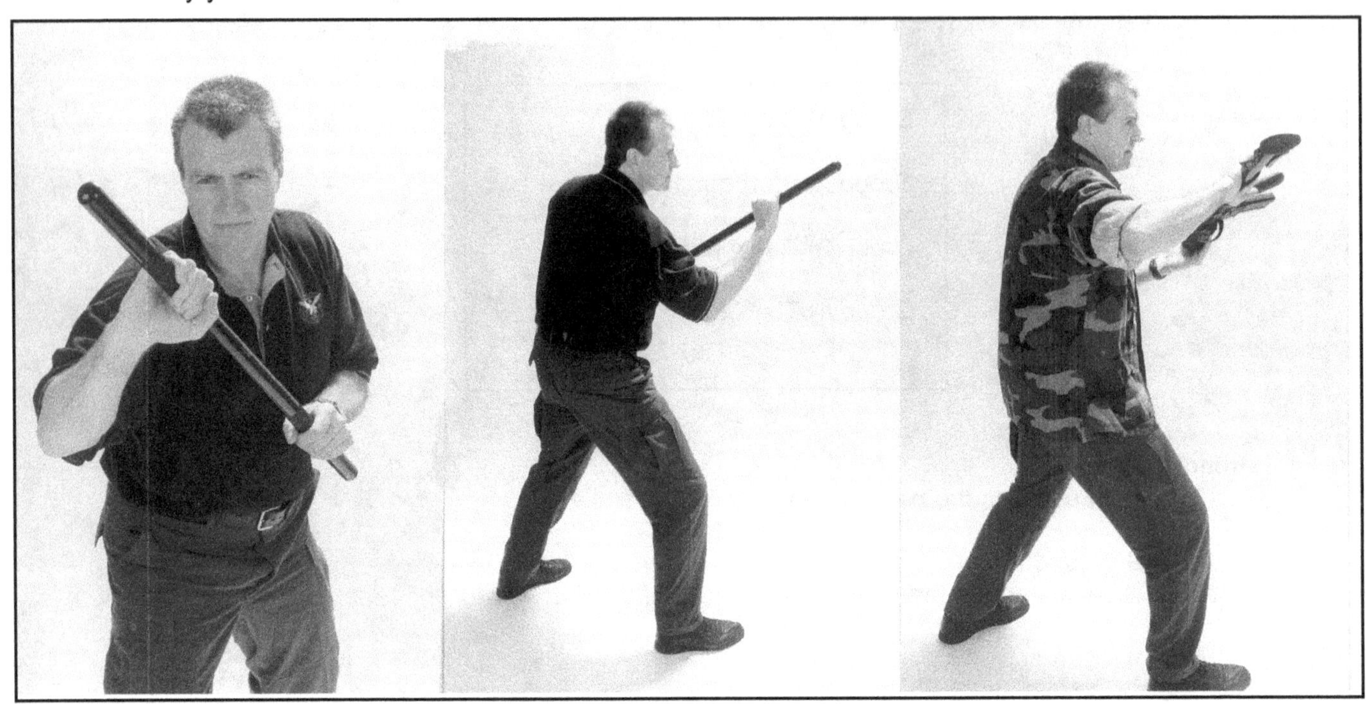

DMS Strike 1) This is a high right side attack.

DMS Strike 2) This is a high left side attack.

DMS Strike 3) Low right side attack.

DMS Strike 4) Low left side attack.

DMS Strike 5) The power shove.

DMS Strike 6) The right side power thrust.

DMS Strike 7) The right side power thrust.

DMS Strike 8) The low left strike.

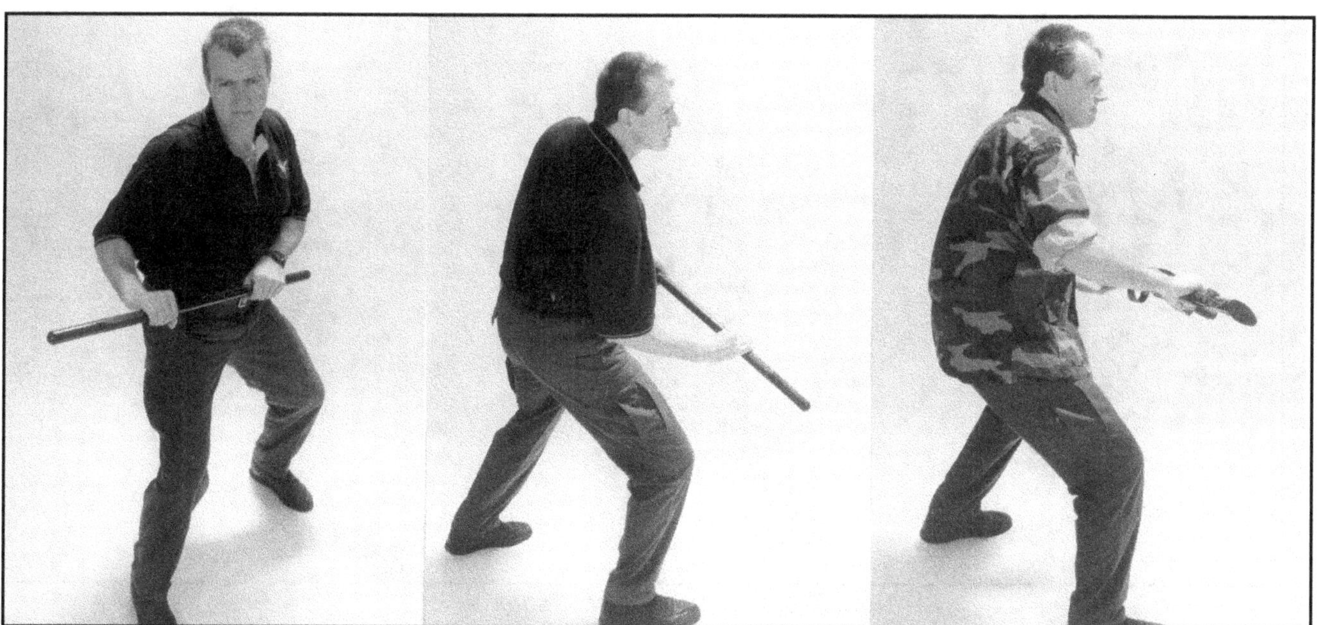

DMS Strike 9) The low right strike.

DMS Strike 10) High right tip hook (Bayonet here) with a subtle follow up of a rear pommel (stock here).

DMS Strike 11) High left tip hook (butt stock here) with follow-up hit of tip (bayonet).

DMS Strike 12) A downward shaft strike.

DMS Strike 13) The forward thrust.

DMS Strike 14) An upward pommel strike or butt stroke.

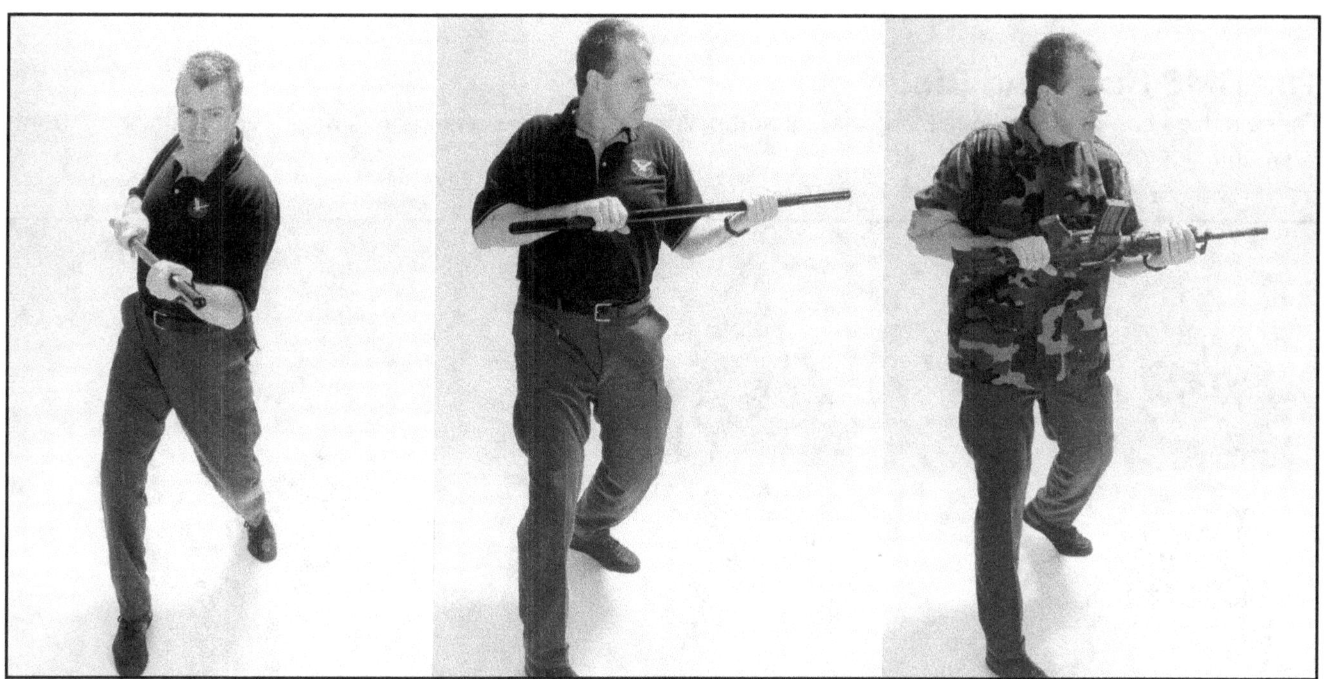

DMS Strike 15) An upward tip or bayonet slash.

Your DMS Summary and Work-out

Practice:
>In the air.
>Hit a training post.
>Exercise these standing.
>Exercise these kneeling.
>Exercise these on your back.

Your workout:

____ 5 Angle 1 strikes
____ 5 Angle 2 strikes
____ 5 Angle 3 strikes
____ 5 Angle 4 strikes
____ 5 Angle 5 strikes
____ 5 Angle 6 strikes
____ 5 Angle 7 strikes
____ 5 Angle 8 strikes
____ 5 Angle 9 strikes
____ 5 Angle 10 strikes
____ 5 Angle 11 strikes
____ 5 Angle 12 strikes
____ 5 Angle 13 strikes
____ 5 Angle 14 strikes
____ 5 Angle 15 strikes

The DMS Surround Riot 4

These strikes can be found in military, martial and police training. The collection is designed to attack the front, back and sides.

*First, draw the weapon. (Review **Training Mission One** for quick draw details.)*

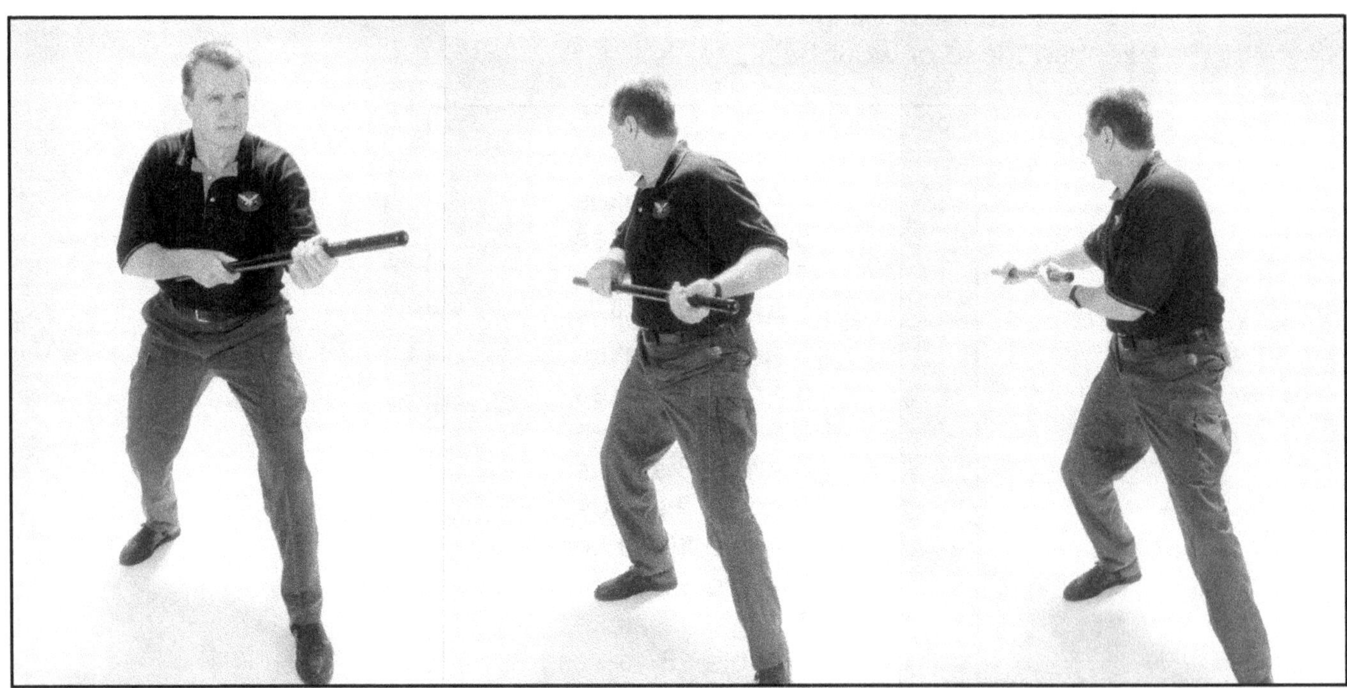

Step 1) Strike forward.   Step 2) Look back.   Step 3) Strike back.

Step 4) Look left.   *Step 5) Strike left.*   *Step 6) Look right.*   *Step 7) Strike right.*

Step 8) Switch leads and look and attack the same sides.

Your DMS Surround Riot 4 Summary and Practice

The Steps:

Step 1) Quick draw.
Step 2) Strike forward.
Step 3) Look back.
Step 4) Strike back.
Step 5) Look left.
Step 6) Strike left.
Step 7) Look right.
Step 8) Strike right.

Practice:

Practice in the air.
Practice standing.
Practice knee-high.
Practice hitting a training object.
    ___ 5 Forward strikes.
    ___ 5 Rear strikes.
    ___ 5 Left side strikes.
    ___ 5 Right side strikes.

Heaven and Hell 4

The enemy is often above and below you. This collection is meant to attack them.

High butt strike.
High stab.

Ground or low butt stroke.
Ground or low stab.

DMS Batting 4

With your two hands on one end of the stick, as if holding a bat or a sword, attack in the four basic clock angles of 12, 3, 6 and 9. Consider leaving a small space between your hands, a common sword technique, that allows for extra control of your weapon. Remember, this grip is only viable with a good-sized stick.

Slash down from high. Slash in from the right side.
Slash up from low. Slash in from the left side.
You may also use the 12 angles of attack as an advanced workout.

Feed the Pommel

While in the act of striking, hooking, or passing, sometimes you need to "feed the pommel," that is shove more stick through your hand until you have enough baton exposed to accomplish your task.

Can't reach the target? In classic staff methodology, push the stick through the lead hand to gain range.

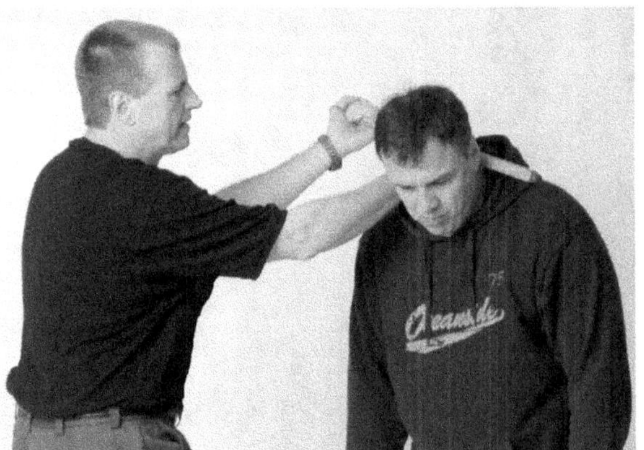

Feed the pommel for a better hook.

For solo command and mastery work, start with a normal DMS grip and shove the stick to the left.

For solo command and mastery work, start with a normal DMS grip and shove the stick to the right.

The Biddle Thrust

In the early 20th century, U.S. Marine Colonel Anthony Drexel Biddle was a pioneer in Marine Corps combatives, forging many ideas from boxing, jujitsu, fencing and other martial systems. One such was this two-hand to one-hand stabbing thrust with a step, perfect for a bayonet stab or a prodding, stick attack.

Starting position DMS strike #13

Let go with the lead hand, step and thrust.
Retract into a combat-ready position.

His view!

The DMS Statue Drill

Throughout the CQC courses we use the so-called statue drill, first introduced in ***Training Mission One*** and reviewed in the prior Unarmed Combatives level of this book. This drill is the foundation for understanding the *point of contact* in combat. New students must be introduced to this full basic training spectrum. The drill ranges from a solid statue, to the trainer taking a few primary attack steps, all in preparation for the student to face chaotic reality.

   Many systems incorporate wooden posts or dummies for this type of training, which has advantages, but all too often training sessions consisting of larger groups will not have such abundant equipment. A live training partner *dummy* provides a suitable facsimile.

Statue Drill Studies and Observations 1) Contact

Contact may come from your strike that is blocked, or from your block defending against a strike. The contact point is a reference point for training. Contact points in an impact weapon encounter may clash:

> Clash 1) Your DMS grip stick to his stick.
> Clash 2) Your DMS stick to his arm.

The basic arms high statue.

Statue Drill Studies and Observations 2) The 2 Basic Possibilities

The study is broken down scientifically to following three possibilities:

> Possibility 1) Stick makes contact and strike strikes.
> > a) any hand strike
> > b) any kick
>
> Possibility 2) Empty hand makes contact and
> > counter strikes with stick.

Statue Drill Studies and Observations 3) The Statue Arms Vary

Depending on the training assignment, the trainer/statue may:

> Trainer Position 1) Have arms straight out and high.
> Trainer Position 2) Have arms bent and low.
> Trainer Position 3) Have arms pumping.
> Trainer Position 4) Steps in and strikes.

The DMS stick statue.

Statue Drill Studies and Observations 4) The Protocol

The SMS drill has 5 trainee body positions:

> Trainee Position 1) Outside of the right arm.
> Trainee Position 2) Inside of the right arm.
> Trainee Position 3) Split between both arms.
> Trainee Position 4) Inside the left arm.
> Trainee Position 5) Outside the left arm.
> Trainee Position 6) Push down his DMS grip and strike.
> Trainee Position 7) Push up his DMS grip and strike.

Statue Drill 1) Stick Contact and Any DMS Follow-Up Stick Strike

Here the stick makes first contact and then the stick quickly strikes. The strike could land anywhere appropriate for the circumstances-neck, face, hand, torso or lower. Here, I work across the body, contacting and striking, starting from the outside, then inside, then the obligatory split movement that reminds practitioners to cover against both arms, then inside, then outside.

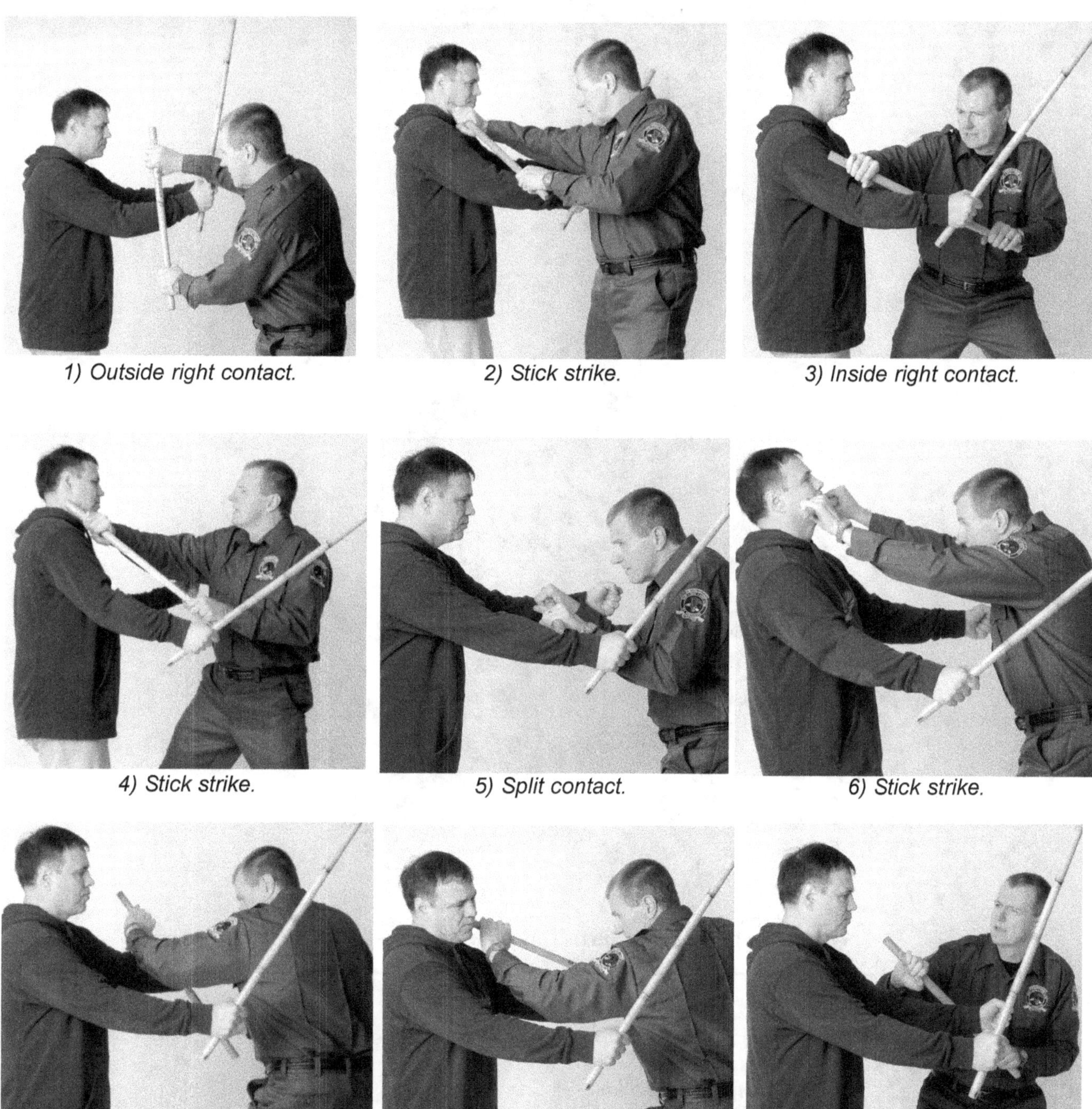

1) Outside right contact.

2) Stick strike.

3) Inside right contact.

4) Stick strike.

5) Split contact.

6) Stick strike.

7) Inside left contact.

8) Stick strike.

9) Outside left contact.

Move freely across the front of the trainer. Mimic a professional sports player with side-to-side footwork. Try not to cross your legs, as this crossover is simply not conducive to mobility. The strike could come from the shaft, tip or handle.

10) Stick strike.

Work the whole series again. This time with lower body strikes.

Practice these training sets.

Basic Set 1) Stick contact and stick strike- work across the body in five sets.
-shaft strikes
-handle/pommel strikes
Basic Set 2) Stick contact and any kick- work across the body in five sets.

Advanced Set 1) Practice these sets on your back. The trainer looms over you.
Advanced Set 2) The trainee charges in, makes contact and strikes in a dynamic manner.
You counter-strike with multiple DMS strikes.

Statue Drill 2) Force Down and Follow-Up Stick Strike

Here your stick makes first contact, slides over the enemy's horizontal DMS grip, and forces the enemy's stick downward. You quickly strike the face.

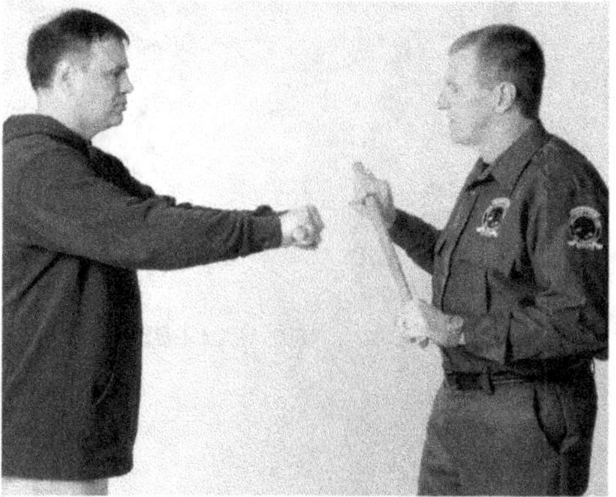

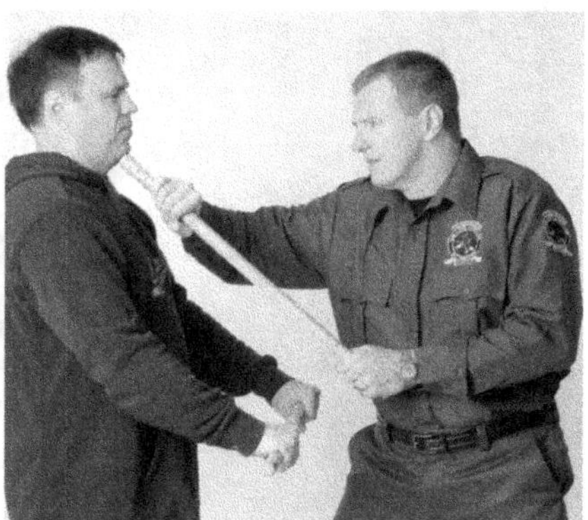

Contact, push the stick down and out of the way, then strike.

Statue Drill 3) Force Up and Follow-Up Stick Strike

Here your stick makes first contact, slides under the enemy's horizontal DMS grip, and your stick forces the enemy's stick upward. You quickly strike the face.

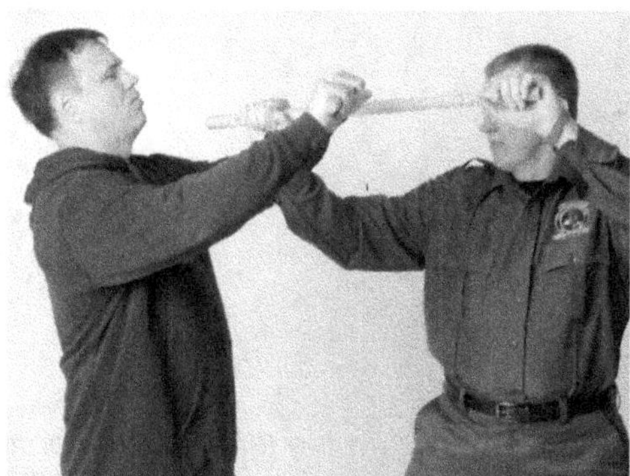
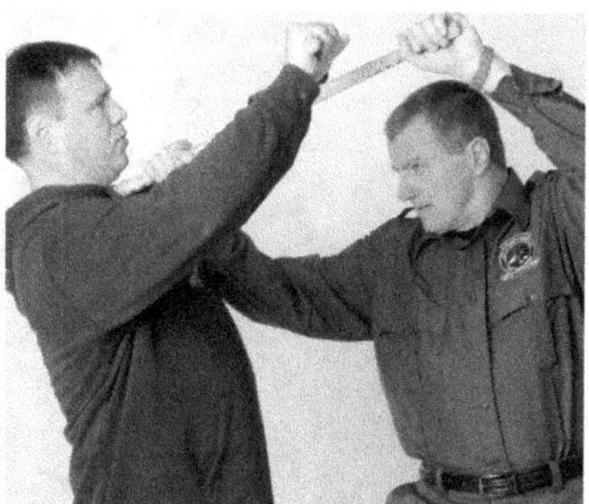

Contact, push the stick up and out of the way, then strike.

Statue Drill 4) Roll-Overs and Roll-Unders

In this statue drill, your statue holds his weapon in a port arms positions. You practice rolling your stick over the top and strike. Next, you roll your stick around the enemy and strike.

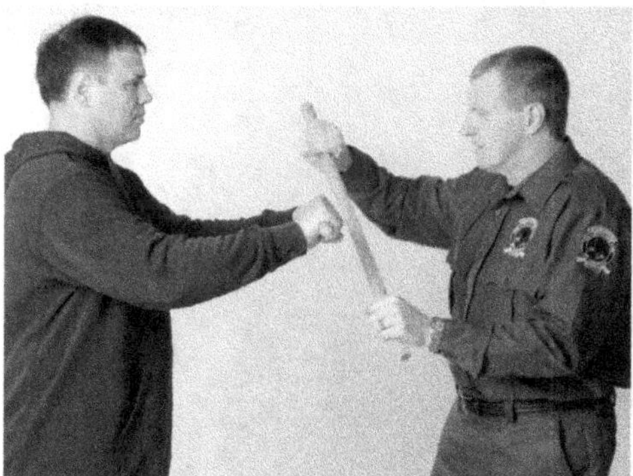
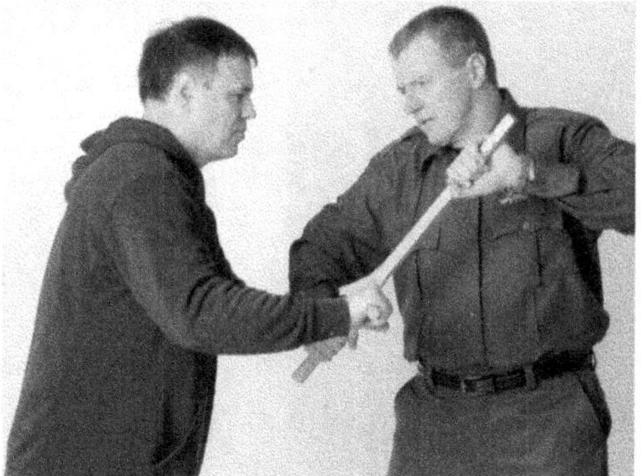
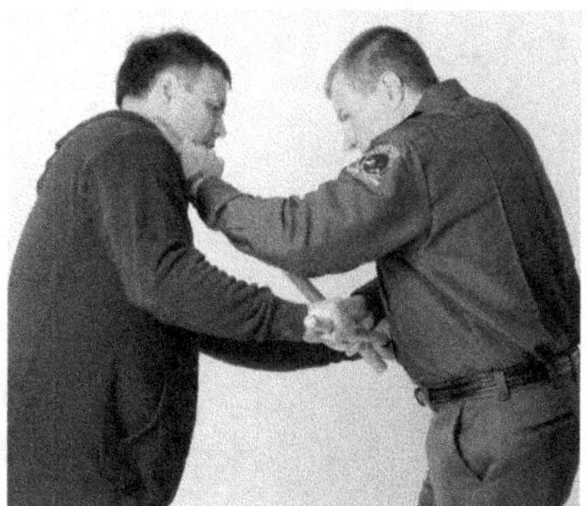

Contact, roll either end of the stick over the top and then strike.

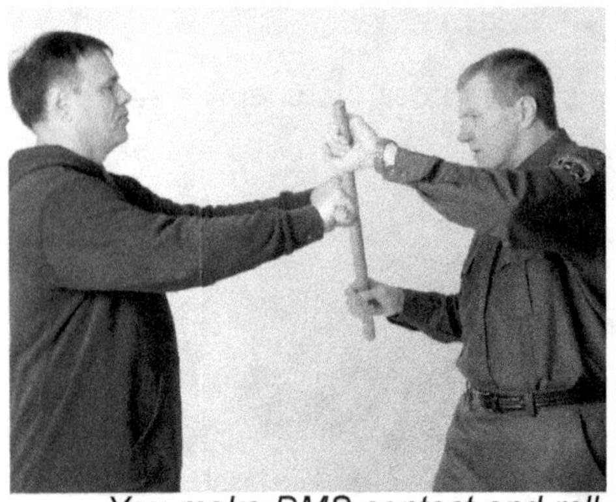

You make DMS contact and roll either end of your stick over the top of the statue stick. Then you strike.

To the left: African forces practice the upward butt stroke.
Above: Think of the many long gun applications.

European protesters go to work, DMS style.

Police officers go to work. How much blocking, striking and grappling stick skills do they really have? The sad answer is, almost none.

DMS Blocking

DMS Split Hand Blocks

*The 12 o'clock or high
DMS two-hand block.*

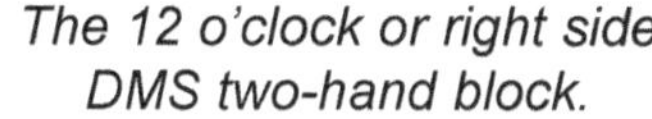

*The 12 o'clock or right side
DMS two-hand block.*

*The 6 o'clock or low
DMS two-hand block.*

*The 9 o'clock or left side
DMS two-hand block.*

DMS Batting Blocks

The high, two-handed block. Your hands could be on the right side or left side.

The right side batting block.

The low, two-handed block. Your hands could be on the right side or left side.

The left side batting block.

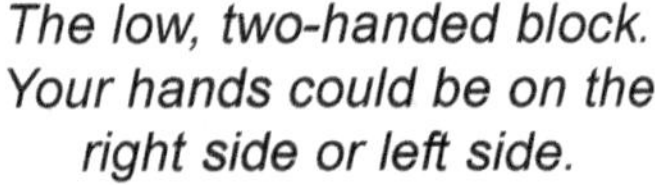

DMS Knee High Maneuver Drill

In close quarter combat, it is imperative to be confident and comfortable maneuvering knee high. If given an opportunity to do so, remaining knee high is usually as low as you should get if an opponent is on his back or chest. Knee high is the superior ground fighting position. Knee high is also the preferred arrest position. Real world combatives are not high school, college and sport judo matches. Of course, you must study these sports also, but to calculate how to defeat the tactics.

In order to enhance these skills, I have organized this knee high drill which I promote with empty hands, impact weapons, pistols, and knives in both saber and reverse grips. For the drill, imagine a clock laid down on the floor and you are at its center, down on both knees.

> You will start by stepping right foot, then left:
> At about the 12 o'clock position, returning to the center.
> At about the 1:30 and 10:30 o'clock positions, returning to the center.
> At about 3 and 9 o'clock positions, returning to the center.
> At about 4:30 and 7:30 o'clock positions, returning to the center.
> At about 6 o'clock positions, returning to the center.

From the center of the clock, or a neutral position...

Step off with the right foot, back to neutral, then to the left foot.

Return to the neutral axis-point of the clock hands.

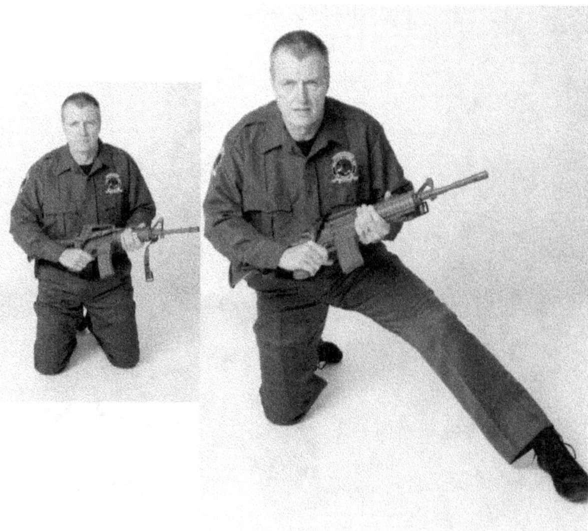

Right foot to 1:30. Then pass through neutral. Left foot to 10:30.

Right foot to 3 o'clock. Then pass through neutral to the left foot to 9:00.

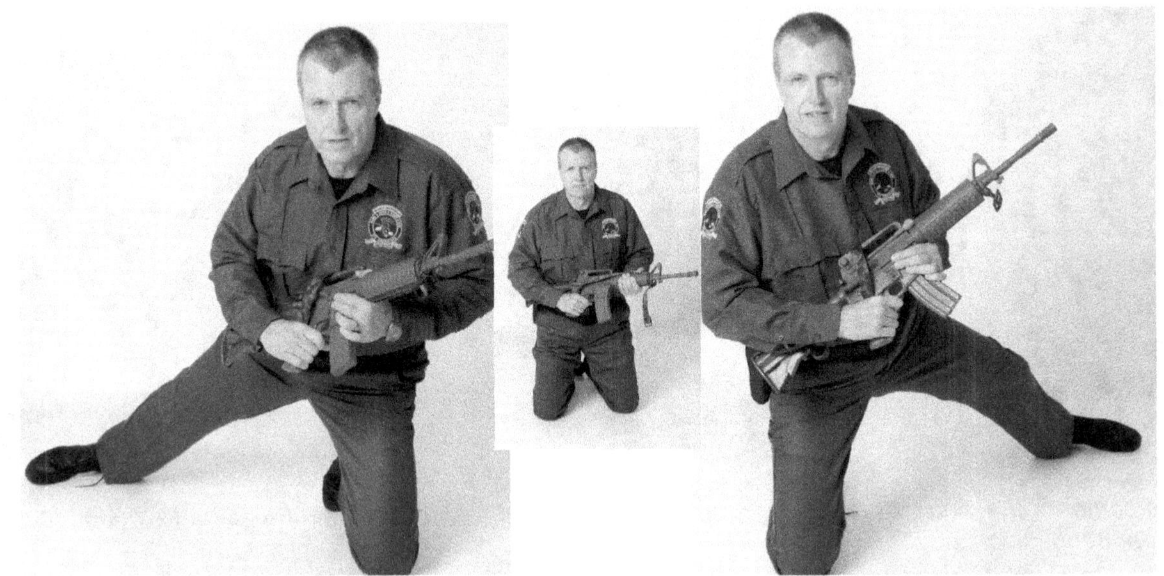

5:30 step. Pass through...   *...to a 7:30 step.*

Then to center. Right foot to 6 o'clock. Left foot to 6 o'clock.

DMS Falling

It is imperative that practitioners learn to fall while brandishing their weapons. Tuck the chin. Round off all corners of the body and expel a bit of air. Be very aware of your weapon, especially if you are brandishing a bayonet on a long gun. A student will tumble:

Fall 1) 12 o'clock or forward- north.
Fall 2) 3 o'clock or to the right- east.
Fall 3) 6 o'clock or to the rear- south.
Fall 4) 9 o'clock or to the left- west.

Get up, and take a quick strike to finish each roll.

Knife/Counter-Knife Combatives
Level 3: The Reverse Grip Slash Module

In ***Training Mission One*** we learned how to quick draw the knife. In ***Training Mission Two*** we learned saber grip slashing. Here we will cover reverse grip slashing on our path to master the science of edged weaponry.

The Reverse Grip Slash Knife Assault Module
The reverse knife grip, so simply put, is when the sharp end of the knife sticks out of the bottom of a hand, in a grip held like an ice pick. A slash of your knife's edge may cause great damage to your enemy, or make only a slight tear in clothing. A slash with a big heavy knife can cause more damage than a smaller, lighter one.

Studies and Observations 1) Review of *Training Mission One and Two*
Vital essentials about knife combatives are documented in ***Training Mission One*** and ***Training Mission Two.*** Review those before proceeding with this segment of training.

Studies and Observations 2) Economy of Motion versus Velocity versus Penetration
Keep the slashing very economical, and in the *window of combat*-that rectangle loosely bordered by your shoulders and upper thighs. The tight, efficient slash comes from the extension of your wrist and movement at the elbow, not shoulder. Too much shoulder and you are giving your opponent a better chance to counter you. Remember that countering your knife slash can take place when you over extend the staging of your slash by rearing your knife back too far, or by slashing your blade too far past your target. Your practice must develop as much velocity as possible inside limited space. Then you must concern yourself with the power of penetration. All these methods may be exercised by striking training objects that you can actually slash into, such as meat, martial training bags and wooden posts.

Knife chambered
and pulled
too far to the rear.

Knife swung too
deep and far past
target.

Studies and Observations 3) The "Apple on a String" Slash
Understand the "apple on a string" impact slashing concept. Strike as if you are hitting into an apple on a string and want to penetrate the apple with your slash as much as possible before the apple bounces away.

Studies and Observations 4) The "Uncommitted Slash"
Understand the "uncommitted slash" theory. You are striking out to hit a particular target, but should there be an obstacle suddenly in the way, you can stop that slash, manipulate and/or redirect the blade to an available target.

Studies and Observations 5) The "Wandering Thumb" Essay

The thumb on the pommel helps fan the blade out and away from your forearm to deliver more power for slash. Then the thumb can rest atop your fingers for a vice-like grip. Let your thumb wander from job to job.

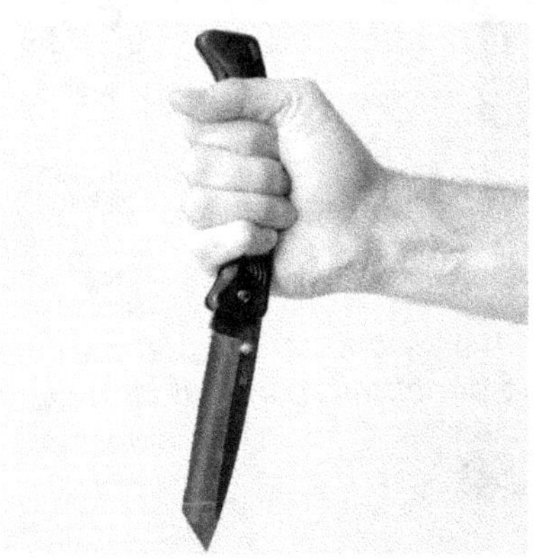

Thumb helping a vice grip.

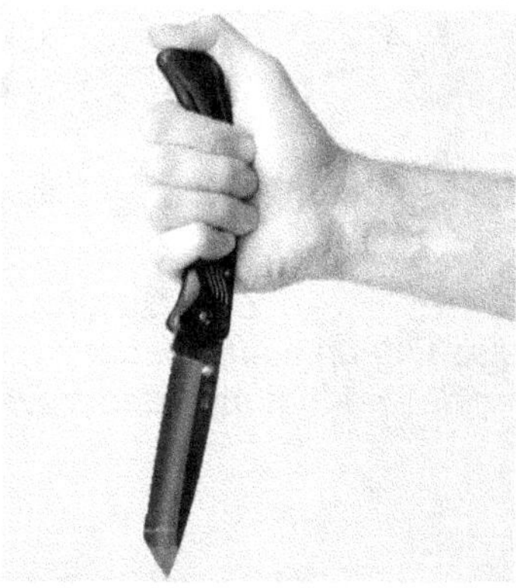

Thumb on pommel.

Studies and Observations 6) The *Slash is not a Knife Block* Awareness

Beware the slashing block. The idea that a slashing knife (or stick) can stop an incoming attack is incorrect. It is so over practiced and misunderstood, I feel the need to include this awareness in the slashing module. A slashing knife may slow an incoming attack only to some degree. The opposing hand, knife or stick may still reach in to cut you. For this awareness drill, a trainer slashes X's at a trainee, deeply. Deep enough to make realistic body contact. The trainee experiments with a saber gripped knife and tries to block the attack. This starts out slowly, then in a resistance continuum, the speed continues. A slash at an incoming attack is not likely to stop it, just slow it down. If the knife is meant to block, do not slash with it.

The knife block must stay and stop the incoming energy, not slash immediately off.

Studies and Observations 7) The Other Hand

Keep the support hand in the window of combat-the rectangle loosely bordered by your shoulders and mid-thighs. The support hand blocks, strikes, grabs, confuses and throws.

Studies and Observations 8) Success of the Slash

Does anyone really need an anatomy lesson on how a knife destroys the body? Suffice to say human life is extremely tenacious. Many victims have survived 30 plus, sometimes over 100 stabs and slashes before death. This alone is not discussed in the training programs of many current martial systems. Civilian and military doctors will report that stabs cause most death, but slashes delivered in the right place can also be serious and deadly. Slashes need to attack main vessels, muscle and nerve lines. The main impediment to slashing is clothing. Military uniforms and load-bearing vests may protect the body to differing degrees. When slashing with a reverse grip, you must punch forward to effect the slash, a movement not needed with saber grip slashing. If you mimic the mechanics of saber slashing with your reverse grip, you will never penetrate the target.

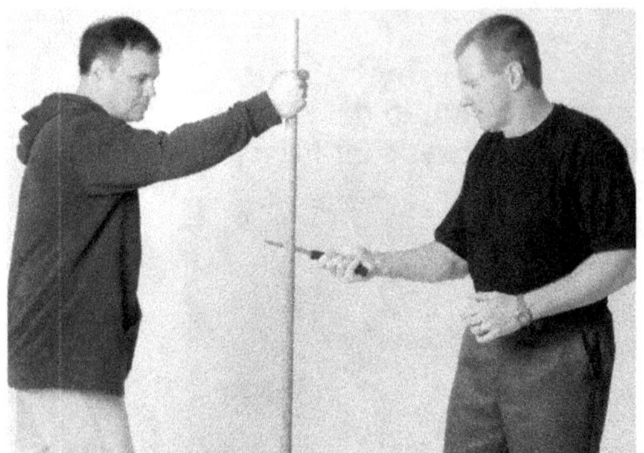

Saber slashing on a stick. Imagine the side-by-side line that my hand travels.

The reverse grip on the same wrist line. No penetration on that same line!

A reverse grip slash requires a forward punching motion (and blade fanning) to have an effect. Arc back.

Studies and Observations 9) Improvisational Edged-Weapons.

If unarmed, what everyday items in your environment, can you snatch to use as a slashing (or stabbing) weapon. If you have some time before impending combat, much can be manufactured. The blades of scissors can be split apart. Items that can hold an edge can be sharpened. Sturdy glass or plastic can be half wrapped with tape or cloth for a handle. A broken glass motel coffee pot, held by the handle, is a weapon. Think about these things.

Studies and Observations 10) Beware the Self-Inflicted Stab!

History is replete with stories of people, once tackled, thrown down or pushed against a wall while holding a knife a reverse grip, stab themselves. It is one of the major unknown problems with the reverse grip of which the inexperienced and naive exponents of that grip are completely unaware. Many of these proponents have falling in love with the *look of a grip* **before** they fell in love with tactical science.

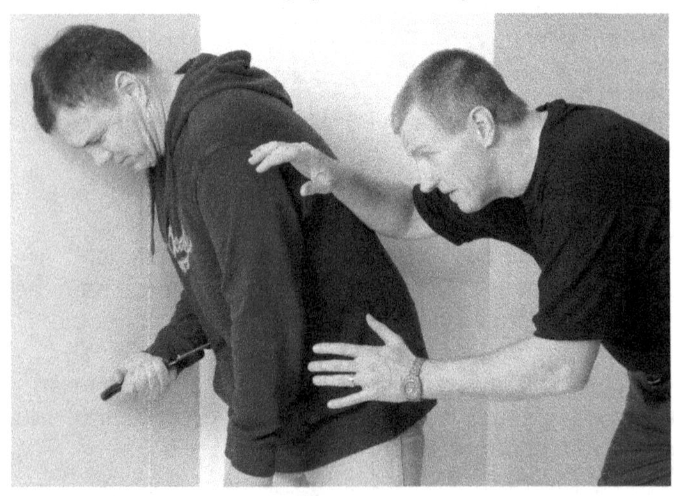

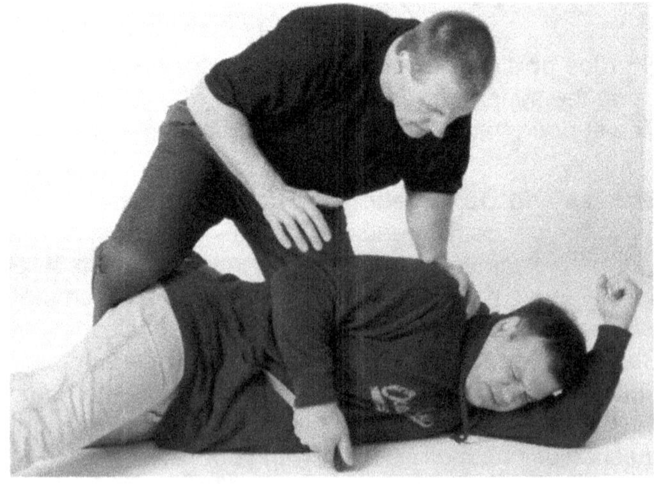

Studies and Observation 11) The RG Wandering Thumb

As shown below, your thumb may wander around the handle as needed. One priority is to use the thumb atop the pommel. This delivers more stabbing power, helps the fanning needed in the slash, and helps keep your hand from sliding down on the blade should your weapon not have a guard/hilt.

Studies and Observations 12) The RG Slashing Push Test

Place your hard training knife against a person. Fan your blade into the person, in an effort to push him back a few inches. That is part of the inertia needed to successfully slash.

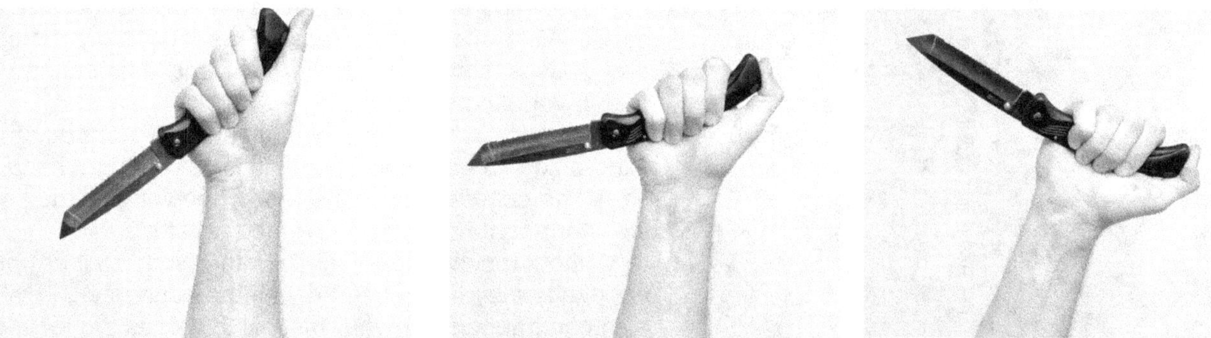

Fanning the blade from your forearm helps insure a successful contact.

Studies and Observations 13) The Curious Edge-in Preference

There are a number of knife experts who prefer the reverse grip over the saber gip and an even smaller grouping selects the edge-in position. They suggest that the knife works best as a sharp gripper, a tool to capture the enemy's arm in a pincher-type approach. They say the edge-in helps cut and control the captured arm.

An even smaller minority suggests that police officers forced to brandish a knife should keep the sharp edge in as a matter of use of force. For them, it seems less offensive if an officer has the dull edge to the enemy. I believe that should an officer be forced to fight with his back-up knife he is in dire straits and would probably need the sharp edge-out advantage.

In the end, most knives are sharp on the second or backside to some degree. In some knife designs 80 percent of the back side is sharp, making the issue virtually moot. Being able to pinch and cut an incoming attack may sound appealing on paper and in slow motion practice, but the simple fact that so many opponents are wearing long sleeve clothing, jackets and parkas, the veracity of the edge-in position may not cut true, or true enough to even bother with this limited position.

The edge-in, reverse grip presentation.

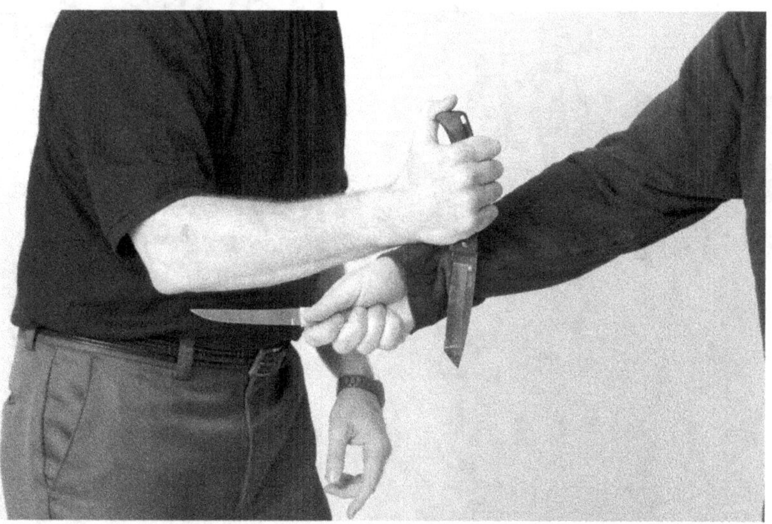

They suggest that the knife works best as a gripper, a tool to capture the enemy's arm in a pincher type approach. They say the edge-in position helps cut and control the captured arm.

You may practice your knife skills with a saber grip, even a reverse grip with its edge facing out, but you may not be aware that the quick draw of your blade under the stress of sudden combat may produce a blade upside down and in reverse of all your practice.

How does this happen? Civilians, hunters, police and military buy and carry their knives, oblivious to steps involved in pulling the weapon. Should they train, the training doctrine of most all knife courses fail to include the most important aspect-getting the knife out under stress. All to often, knife practitioners, especially martial arts classes, start their training sessions knife in hand, in their favorite position.

A standard sheath that accompanies a store bought fixed-blade knife will be form-fitting. For the right hand belt carry, the edge will be to the rear when you pull the knife with your right hand (as shown to the left).

Without much preparation, whether you like it or not, your knife may be presented with the edge back. This also can happen with your tactical folder, as the location of the clip on the folder will dictate the sharp-edge's final position.

An ambidextrous sheath, shown below, can be purchased that frees you to position your fixed blade edge in or out, right or left handed grips and carries.

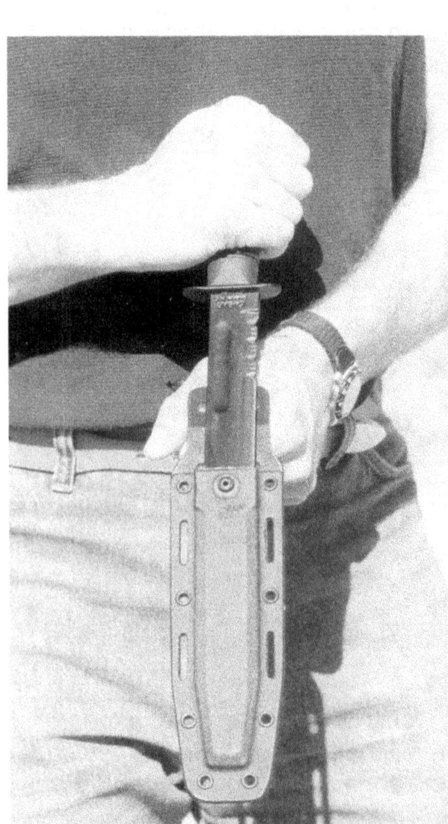
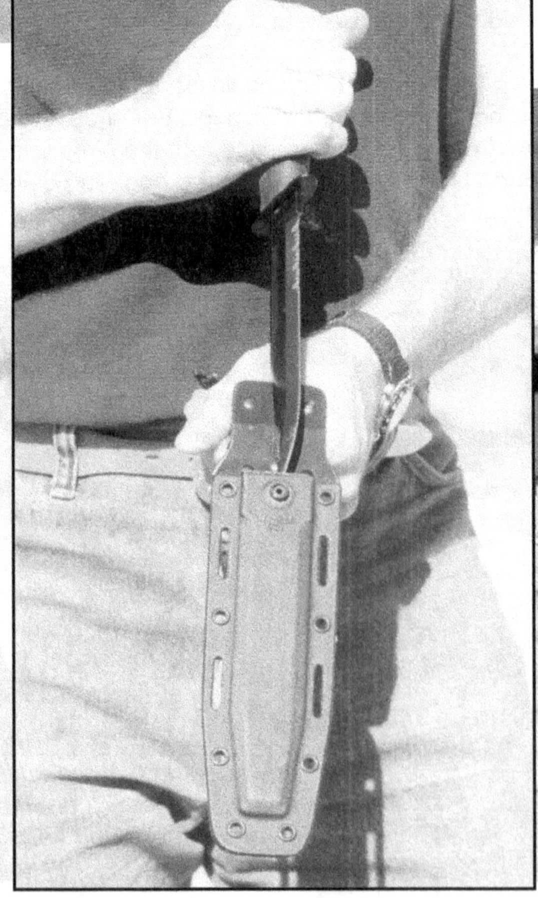
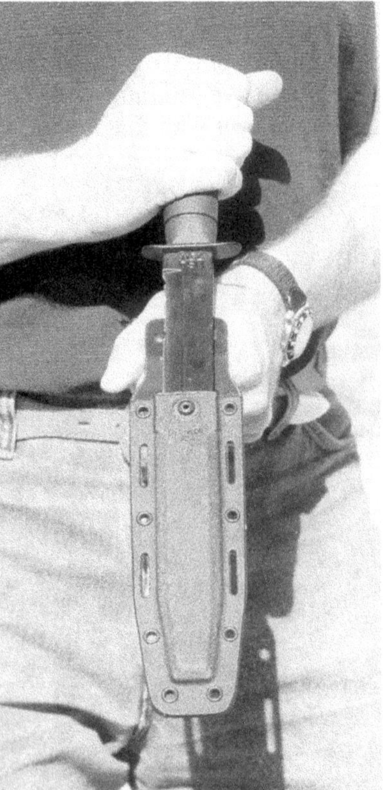

"The best swordsman in the world doesn't need to fear the second best swordsman in the world; no, the person for him to be afraid of is some ignorant antagonist who has never had a sword in his hand before; he doesn't do the thing he ought to do, and so the expert isn't prepared for him; he does the thing he ought not to do; and often it catches the expert out and ends him on the spot."

--Mark Twain

Knife Reverse Grip Slash Solo Command and Mastery

The Basic Single Slash Drills: Learn the essence of reverse grip (RG) slashing with these drills. We all recall the clock training patterns from the prior Mission books, so there is no need to demonstrate them all here again here. Instead, we demo the standing, kneeling and ground positions to slash from.

RG Slash Drill 1) Introduction to the Single Reverse Grip Slash:
Basic 4 slashes: Execute on the four corners of the clock, being 12-ish (or high), 3, 6, 9.
Advanced 9 clock slashes: Execute a single slash for each angle, or number of the clock.

- The right hand slash comfortably covers 11 to 9 o'clock. (angles 10, 11 and 12 feel impractical)
- The left hand slash comfortably covers 3 to 11 o'clock. (angles 12, 1 and 2 feel impractical)
- Do these standing, walking, kneeling and on the ground, right-handed and left-handed.

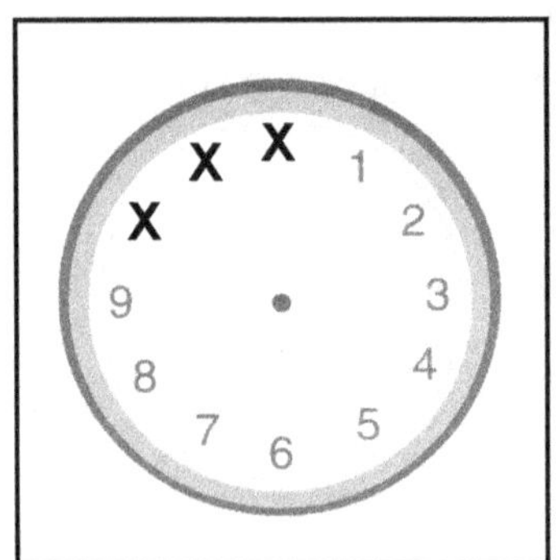

Right-handed, reverse grip slashing is awkward at the 10, 11 and 12 clock angles.

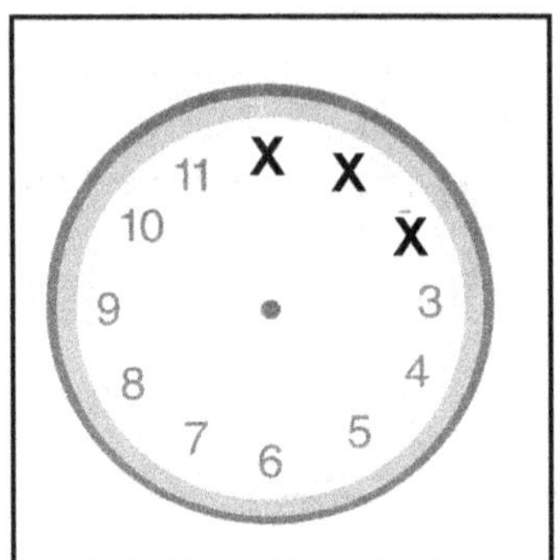

Left-handed, reverse grip slashing is awkward at the 12, 1 and 2 clock angles.

RG Slash Drill 2) Support Strikes
Before or after the slash, you either hand strike or kick. Overuse the knife. The knife is a great equalizer, but it is not God's gift to equalization. You must use your entire body to fight.

1/2 beat hand strike.

1/2 beat kick.

RG Slash Drill 3) The Double Slash

The double slash involves a follow-up cut that returns more or less on the same line as the original slash. Given the problems with the limited angles of RG slashing, it becomes impractical to slash with X patterns. Double slashing may be as good as it gets.

Anatomy of a RG double slash. Here the sample shows a palm down across and palm up back.

RG Practice:

The Basic Training 4 corner version with each:
- slash downward from the high-11 or 1 o'clock.
- slash across from 3 o'clock.
- slash up from 6 o'clock.
- slash across from 9 o'clock.

The Advanced Training version:
- right hand grip-slash from 1 to 9 o'clock angles.
- left hand grip-slash from 3 to 11 o'clock angles.

Double slashing on approximately the same line.

The clock numbers with any ½ beat hand strike.

The clock numbers with any ½ beat kick.

The Reverse Grip Knee High Knife Ground Clock Drill

It is vital that a practitioner is comfortable maneuvering knee high and while holding a knife. If given an opportunity to do so, remaining knee high is usually as low as one should get if an opponent is on his back or chest. Knee high is the superior ground fighting position. It is where you can deliver hand, fore-arm, elbow and knee strikes. For enforcement and correction officers, the knee high is also the preferred arrest position. Real world combatives are not high school, college and sport judo matches. Of course, you must study the lower wrestling levels too, but to calculate how to defeat the tactics.

In order to enhance these skills, I have organized this knee high drill which I promote with empty hands, impact weapons, pistols, and knives in both saber and reverse grips. For the drill, imagine a clock laid down on the floor and you are at its center, down on both knees. You will start by stepping right foot, then left.

Follow the same ground clock steps you have seen in prior
***TM** books and earlier in this publication.*

Practice:

-at about the 12 o'clock position, returning to the center.
-at about the 1:30 and 10:30 o'clock positions, returning to the center.
-at about 3 and 9 o'clock positions, returning to the center.
-at about 4:30 and 7:30 o'clock positions, returning to the center.
-at about 6 o'clock positions, returning to the center.

Reverse Grip Killshot Knife Sparring

Too much Dueling! But still we must do some. Two opponents, squaring off for a duel is an event least likely to occur in our modern world. Yet, this 19th century model preoccupies most of contemporary edged weapon training. Yes, a face-off, showdown duel still can occur, so this range of small conflict must be studied, but not at the expense of other more like CQC events. Here, we endeavor to document some "dueling/sparring" for both the experience and exercise. Never forget that real duelers must cheat in this face-off, grabbing and/or using ANYTHING near them to get the edge. Pick up something to use as a battering ram or a shield.

Also, I have trained many military specialists who require dueling strategies and tactics. They report to me that at times they are advancing into tunnels and caves smelling of explosives and incendiary fluids. Fearful of firing their weapons in such a volatile environments, they are often left with knives up and ready to fight. The science of dueling must be passed on for these exceptional circumstances.

Face-off dueling can happen in the real world, so you must train for the possibility.

Slash Sparring is a footwork enhancer, as well as to learn the harsh realities of the duel, should that event happen to you! Plus, dedicating sessions to reverse grip sparring is a learning experience. Many practitioners finish with the session and decide never to spar in a real fight with a reverse grip, opting instead for a saber grip.

In Killshot training, wear as much body protection as possible, especially eye cover, fight with soft training knives. Work one minute rounds:

Rounds of right versus right.
Rounds of left versus left.
Rounds of left versus right.
Rounds of right versus left.
Rounds of double knife versus double knife.
Rounds of single versus double knife.
Rounds of knee-high versus knee-high, any grip.
Rounds of ground side-by-side, any grip.
Rounds of short knife versus long knife and/or machete.
Rounds of unarmed versus knife.

Start these rounds anyway you wish. Four main ideas?
Round Starter 1) Armed and facing off.
Round Starter 2) Armed and back-to-back.
Round Starter 3) Knives in sheathes, pocketed or otherwise closed.
Round Starter 4) Knives tossed on the ground.

"...dedicating sessions to reverse grip sparring is a learning experience. Many practitioners finish the session and decide never to spar in a real fight with a reverse grip, opting instead for a saber grip."

Slashing the Statue Drill

The Close Quarters Combatives Group uses the statue drill extensively, introduced in *Training Mission One,* as a method of bridging new practitioners from practicing in the air, to making physical contact with opponents. It also reminds the experienced practitioner of vital tactics and strategies. In this drill we practice contacting the limbs of our trainer and striking. Remember, we used a still statue, and then a pumping statue, to wean the student into more realistic contact. You will also learn the pivot maneuver just to develop more skill. Against the arms of the statue, there are three practice options:

> Option 1) The knife makes arm contact and then moves to slash the throat.
> Option 2) The empty hand makes arm contact and the knife moves in to slash the throat.
> Option 3) Both hands make arm contact, then the knife moves in to slash the throat.

The Statue Pattern) Outside, inside, split, inside, outside

This drill introduces a practitioner to the applications of slash attack and cultivates an ambidextrous ability previously not cultivated. The repetition also de-sensitizes the practitioner to knife violence. The statue's arms can be in high, low and mixed positions. The arms can pump. The arms can be punched forward with a step.

Knife Makes First Contact...

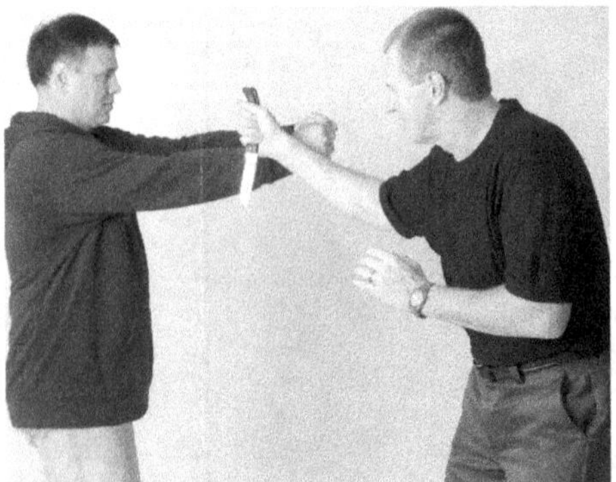

Outside arm knife contact.

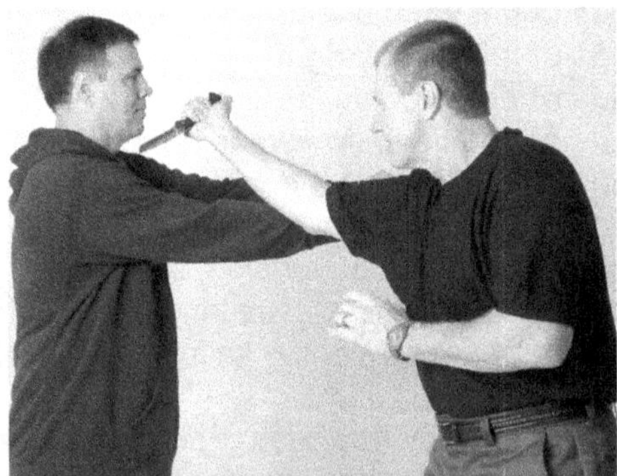

The knife slashes to a target.

Inside arm contact.

Knife slashes.

Split arm contact.

Knife slashes.

Inside arm contact.

Knife slashes.

Outside arm contact.

Knife slashes.

Hand Makes First Contact...

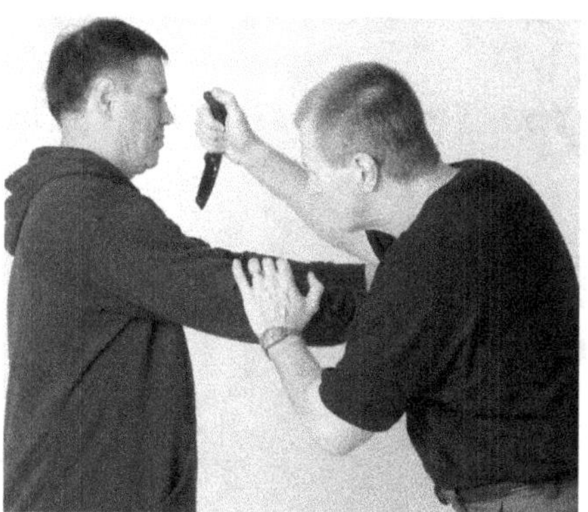

Hand contact and knife strikes.

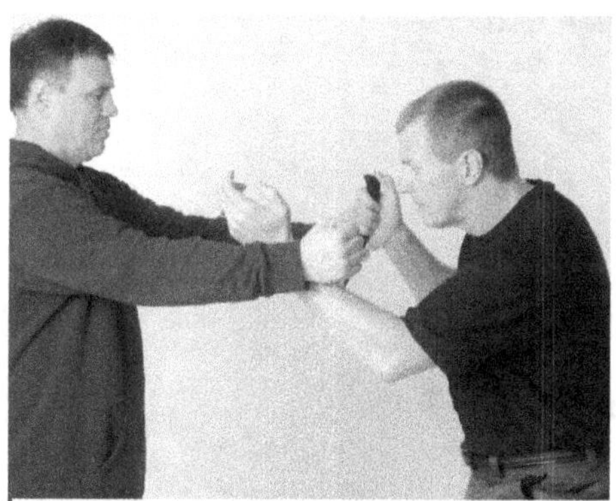

Inside right arm contact.

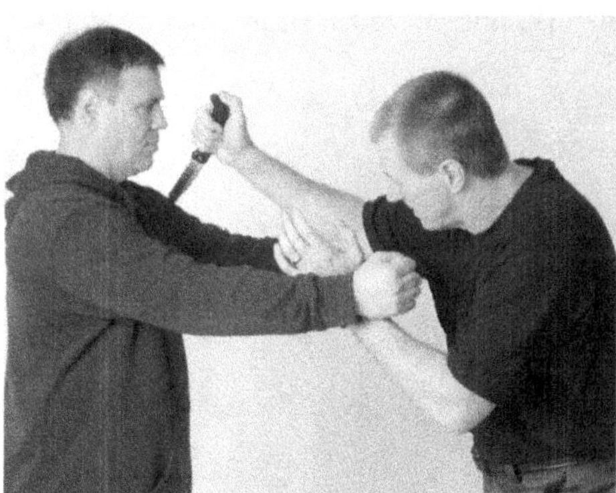

Knife attacks.

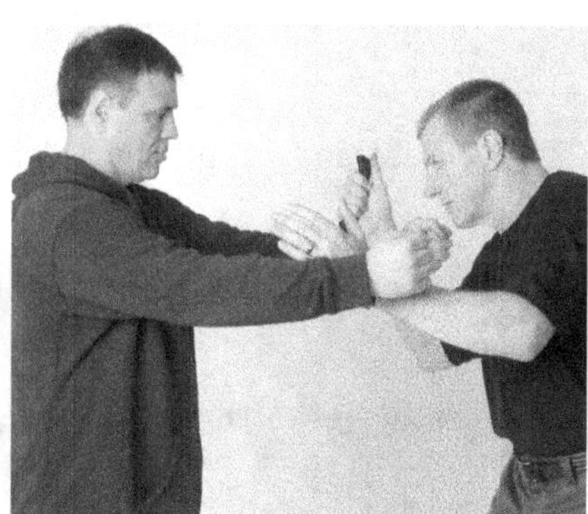

Double arm contact.

Knife strikes.

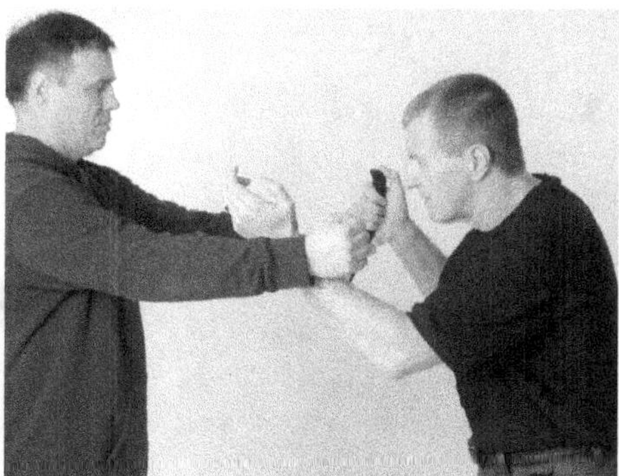

Inside arm contacts left arm.

Knife strikes.

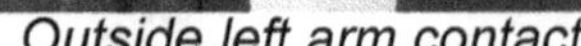

Outside left arm contact.

Knife strikes.

Your Reverse Grip Knife Slash Statue Drill Practice

Session 1) The knife makes arm contact and moves to slash the throat. Change targets at will.

Session 2) The empty hand makes arm contact, and the knife moves in to slash the throat.

Session 3) Both hands make arm contact, and the knife moves in to slash the throat.

Session 4) Vary the statue arm positions. Both high. Both low. Split high and low.

Session 5) You have a right-handed knife.

Session 6) You have a left-handed knife.

Session 7) The trainer pumps the arms to give the trainee a sense of attack.

Session 8) The trainer steps and strikes into the positions previously practiced.

The Principles of Reverse Grip Knife Blocking

Using the clock format, and usually using a thumb up capped atop the pommel for extra support, here are the major reverse grip blocks.

High, 12 o'clock block. Tip in or out.

Right side, 3 o'clock.

Low, or 6 o'clock. Tip in or out.

Left side, 9 o'clock.

Sweep under the clock. Right and left sweeps.

Always try to snatch up a blocking tool. ALWAYS!

Principles in Unarmed Blocking versus the Knife

Using the clock format, these are the major blocks of the unarmed combatant versus the knife attacker. Note that the tender insides of the arm are turned inward. Layers of clothing and special hard protective equipment may help protect the limb. The block is a reflexive act, often to protect vital body zones such as the face and neck. All slashes are bad, however we try to minimize wounds. If possible, always grab something nearby to block and fight with it. Unarmed blocking is a last resort.

12 o'clock.

3 o'clock block.

6 o'clock block.

9 o'clock block.

The tip of the knife can be aimed either way. This will depend on your position just before the block.

Common clothing can really add protection to your limbs and body. I have an expression, "What you can do successfully on the hot Pacific Islands 12 months out of the year, you cannot do in Minnesota 6 months of the year. Sweatshirts! Jackets! Clothing!"

Counters to Common Blocks Study

You've seen the slashing strikes. You've seen the armed and unarmed blocks. Next we have drill and skill developing sets to counter common blocks, all done in the same spirit as a football team running tires or running pass plays to develop their sharp turns and ball-catching skills. Isolate and drill important steps to hone performance. Start by practicing against an unarmed trainer, then eventually-an armed trainer, who throws up common reflexive blocks against your attacks. They are just knife manipulation drills. Here are the clock attack points and the common blocks for this CCB drill:

The Four Counters to Common Blocks

I have identified the four main ways to counter the enemy's block thrown up against your aggressive advance. They are as follows:

> Counter 1) Fake. A good fake sends the block out of your intended path.
> Counter 2) Cut the block after to make contact.
> Counter 3) Re-direct your thwarted attack on another open line.
> Counter 4) Invading hands. Use your support hand to:
> -pin the block
> -pass the block
> -push the block
> -pull the block
>
> (For clarity and real time demonstration, see all these in
> ***Training Mission Three: the DVD***.)

Counter to Common Blocks 1) The Fake sample

Attack convincingly on any line of attack. Observe the blocking reaction, then slash in on any opening you have just created with your fake.

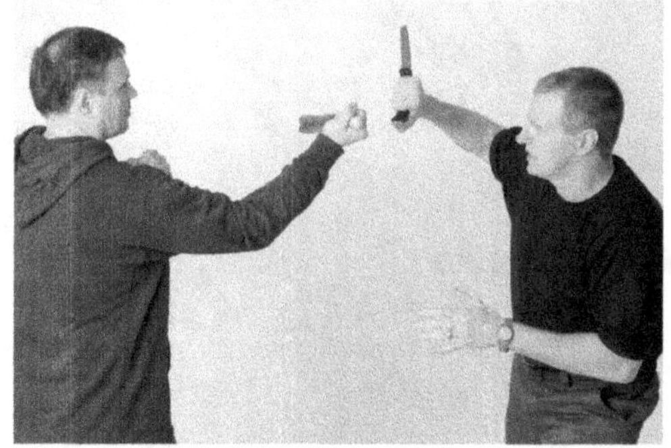

Counter 1: The fake. Make it look good!

> Practice:
> Fake on 1 o'clock, slash on 9 o'clock.
> Fake on 3 o'clock, slash on 12 o'clock.
> Fake on 6 o'clock, slash on 3 o'clock.
> Fake on 9 o'clock, slash on 12 o'clock.
> Practice with the opposite hand.

Counter to Common Blocks 2) Cut the Block sample

Attack convincingly on any line of attack. Observe the blocking reaction, then slash the blocking limb, especially if no other targets are reachable.

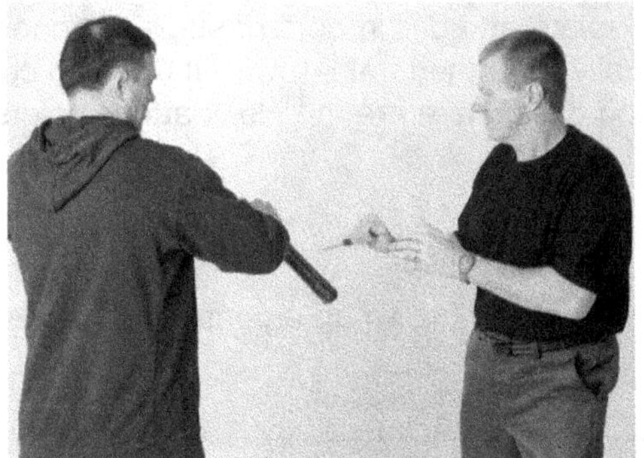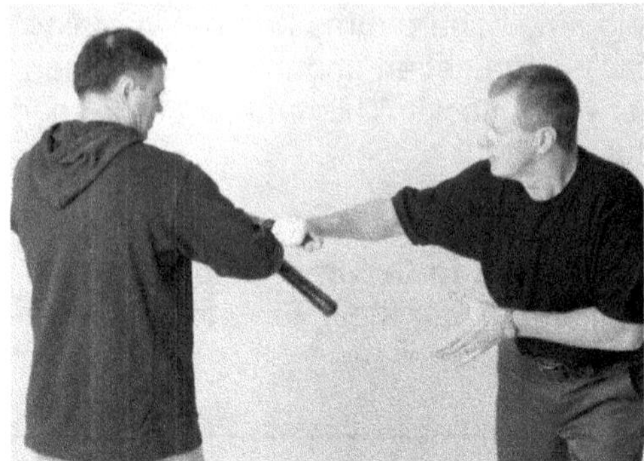

Counter 2: Cut the blocking limb, especially when you cannot reach another target.

Practice:
>Attack on 1 o'clock, cut the block.
>Attack on 3 o'clock, cut the block.
>Attack on 6 o'clock, cut the block.
>Attack on 9 o'clock, cut the block.
>Practice with the opposite hand.

Counters to Common Blocks 3) Re-Direct the Attack on Another Line sample

The block has made contact. Manipulate the knife into another attack. You can see the block coming into your path? Settle for a cut on the blocking limb. Or, after limb to limb contact has been made, make a quick cut on the block.

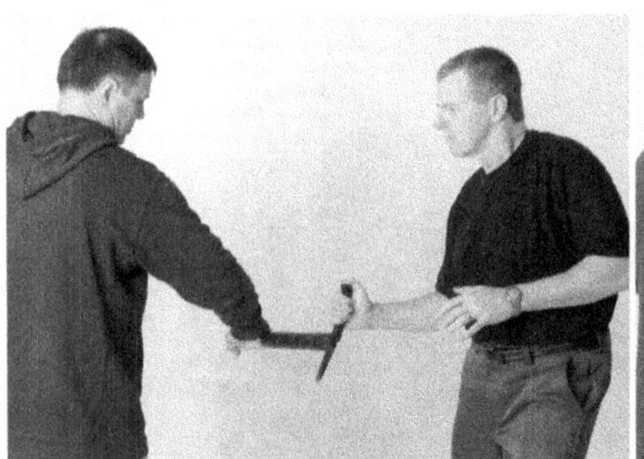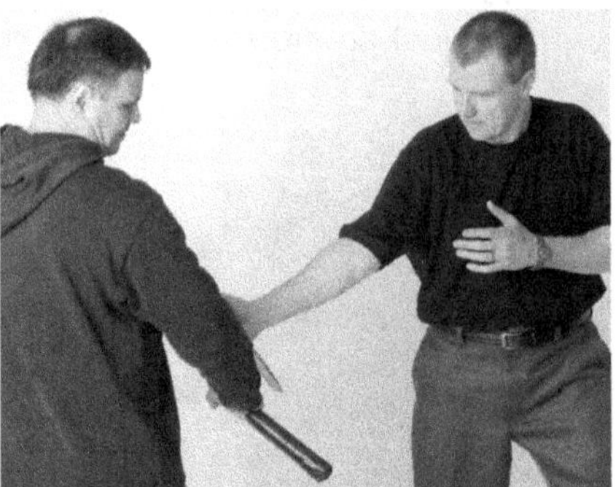

Counter 3: You strike, see the block coming, and assault on another line.

Practice:
>Attack on 1 o'clock, redirect an attack on another line.
>Attack on 3 o'clock, redirect an attack on another line.
>Attack on 6 o'clock, redirect an attack on another line.
>Attack on 9 o'clock, redirect an attack on another line.
>Practice with the opposite hand.

Counters to Common Blocks 4) Invading Hands sample

The block has made contact. Using your hands to pin, pass, push or pull the blocking limb to clear a path to a better target.

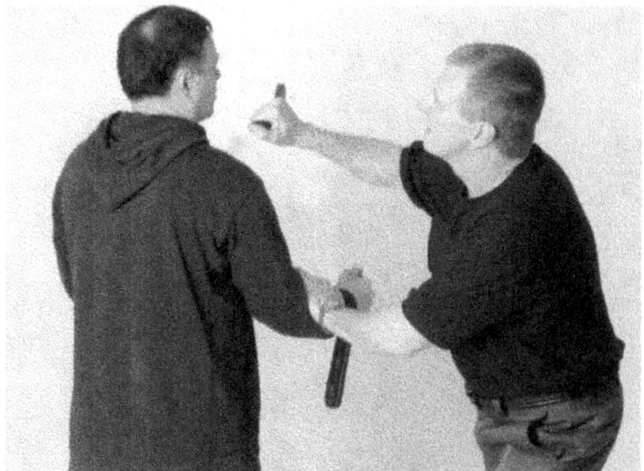

You strike, hit the block, and slap the arm out of the way. The knife continues in.

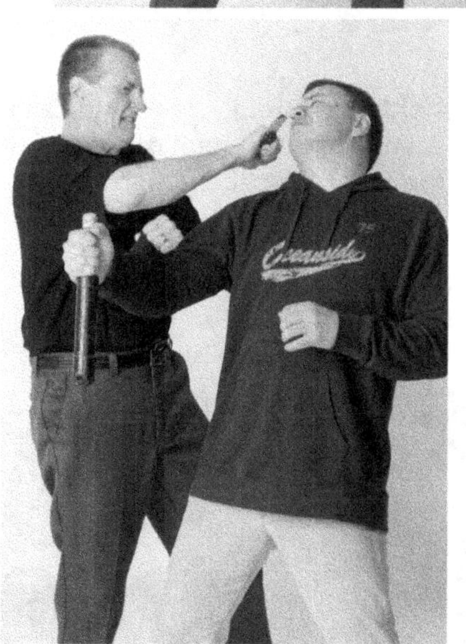

Practice:
        Attack on 1 o'clock, invade in with the four P's.
        Attack on 3 o'clock, invade in with the four P's.
        Attack on 6 o'clock, invade in with the four P's.
        Attack on 9 o'clock, invade in with the four P's.
        Practice with the opposite hand.

The Reverse Grip Slash Block, Pass and Pin Drill

As a veteran of *Training Mission One* book and DVD, you should know the 6 main beats/steps of this popular skill drill. This will teach great speed, manipulation and target acquisition.

Block

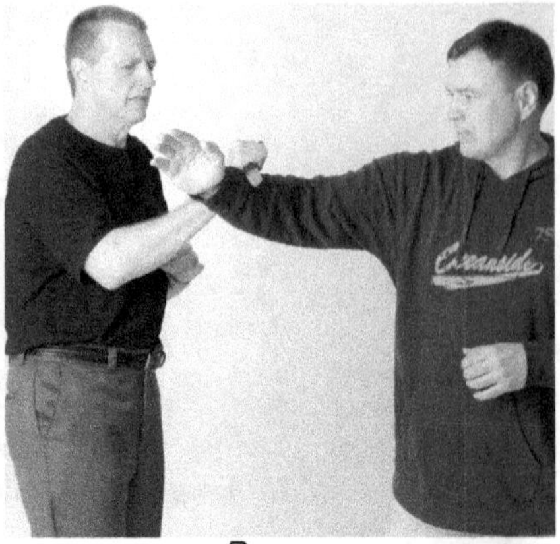

Pass

Pin

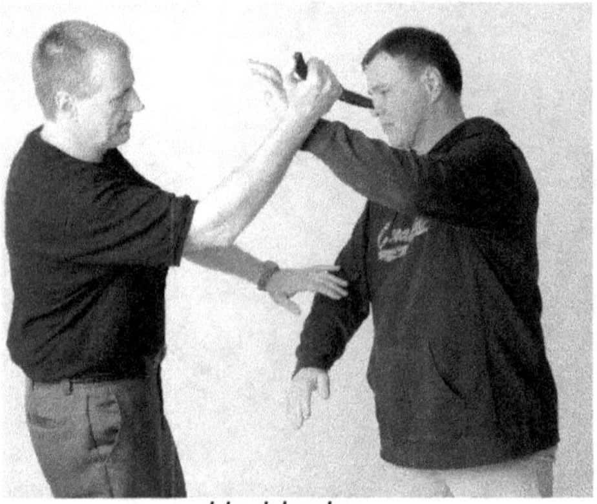

He blocks.

He passes.

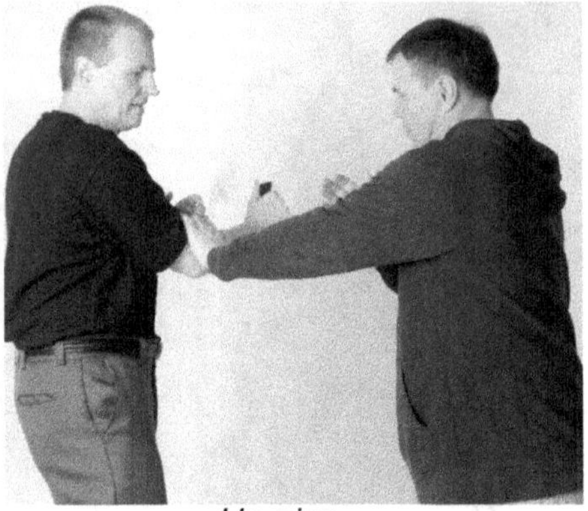

He pins.

1/2 Beat Slashing Inside the Block, Pass and Drill

After a few practice rounds of this 6 beat drill, start inserting 1/2 beat slashes, the subject of this module. Good practice targets are the lower arm, the upper arm and the throat.

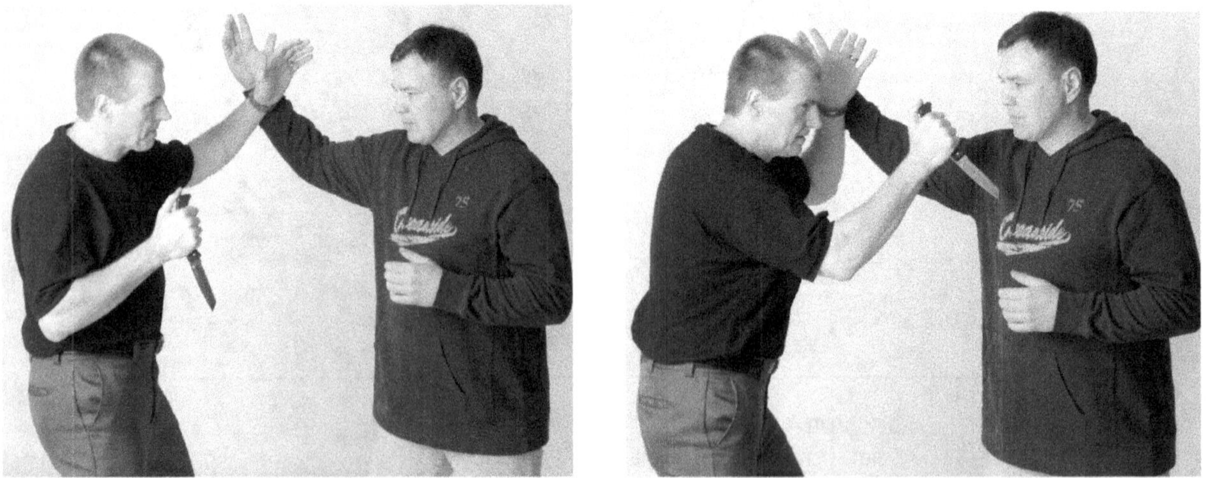

Beat 1 and 1/2: You block. The weapon arm strikes the best available target.

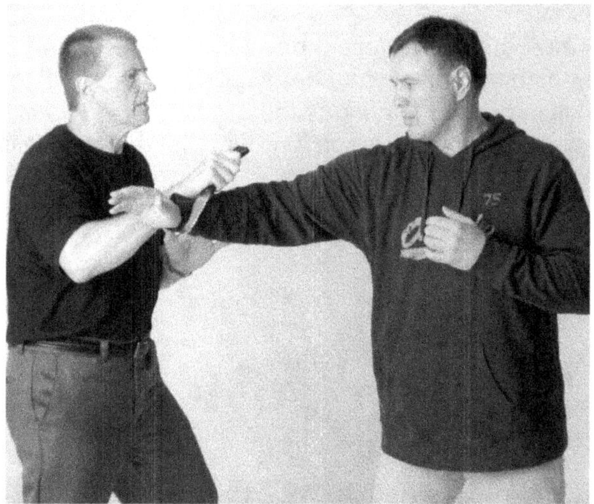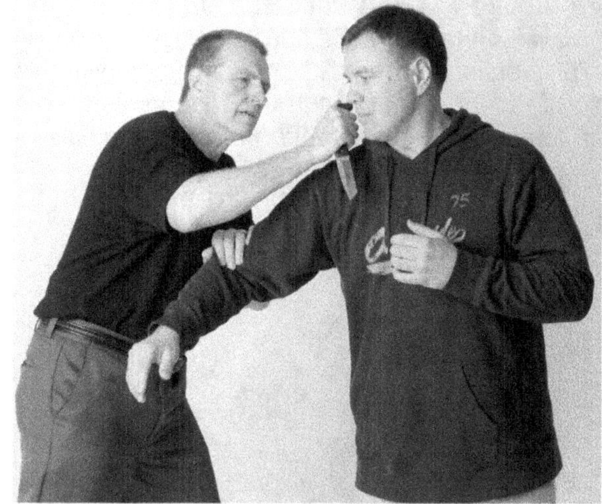

Beat 2 and 1/2: You pass, hook the arm and strike the best available target.

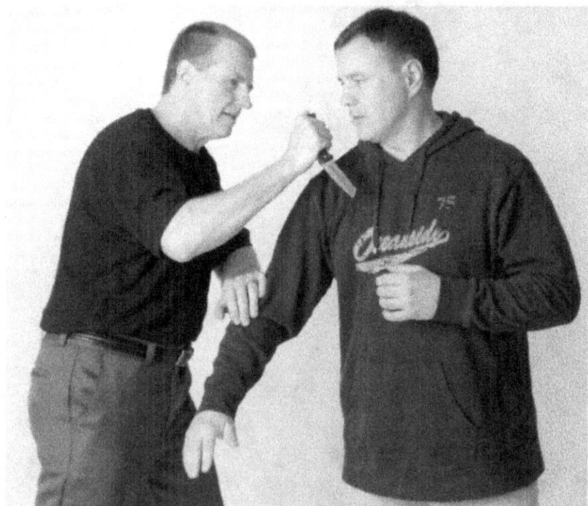

Beat 3 and 1/2. You pin the arm and strike the best available target.

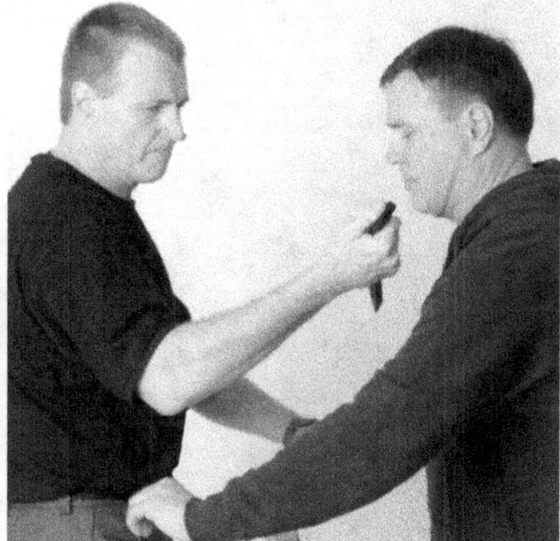

*Beat 4 and 1/2: He blocks. You hook the arm, pull down to clear a path,
then rocket the knife forward to the best target.*

The block, pass and pin format exists only to insert tactics in the half-beats or half-steps to isolate and develop specific skills. The initial attack can come from the high right, high left, low right and low left. Since our subject matter is the saber slash, we will insert these slashes on the half beats. Remember, do not become a drill expert. Instead become a fighting expert. Use just enough drills to develop good skill. Do not over emphasize drills at the expense of combat scenario expertise.

The Leg Block Pass and Pin Slash Drill

Often you will be faced with the kicking legs of your enemy after they have fallen, or after you have taken them down. This version of the drill familiarizes you with this knee-high versus prone enemy position. The drill teaches related knife-to-leg-target acquisition. Remember a major skill in ground fighting is moving *or making your arms like your legs, your legs like your arms.* This drill also enhances Randy Roberson's ground fighting leg skills.

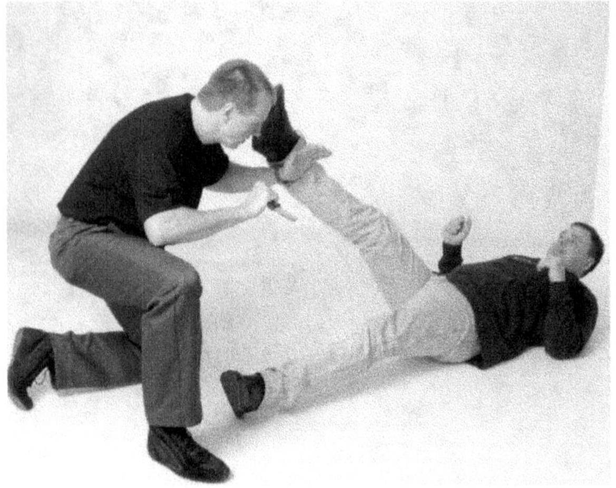

Block the leg.

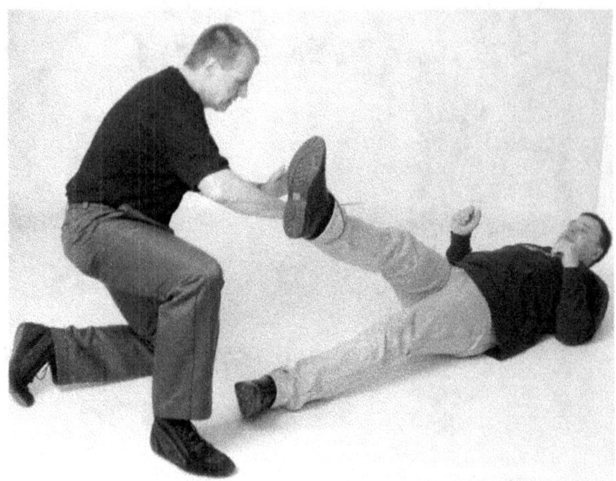

Pass the leg.

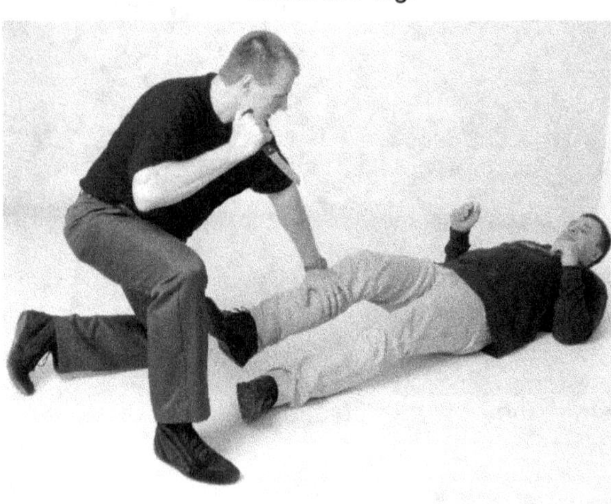

Pin the leg.

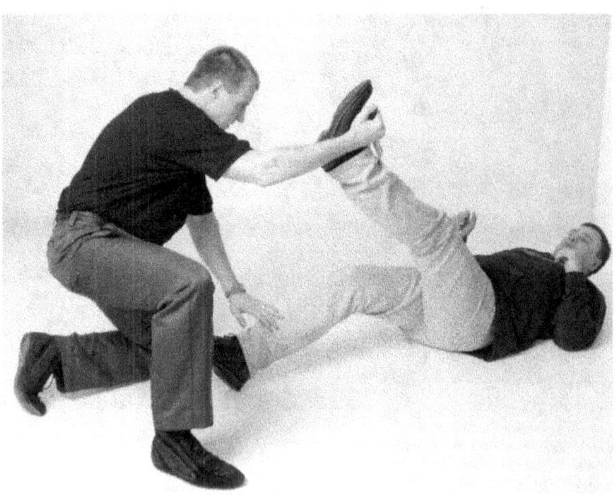

He blocks the attack.

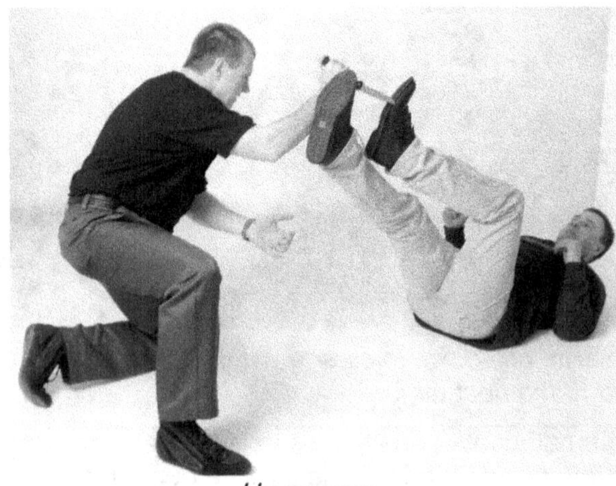

He passes.

He pins.

Make your arms your legs, and make your legs your arms.

1/2 Beat Leg Slashing Inserts Inside the Block, Pass and Drill

After a few practice rounds of the 6 beat drill, start inserting 1/2 beat slashes. Good practice targets are the lower leg, the upper leg and the groin. Cut them on beat 1 and 1/2 for this drill practice.

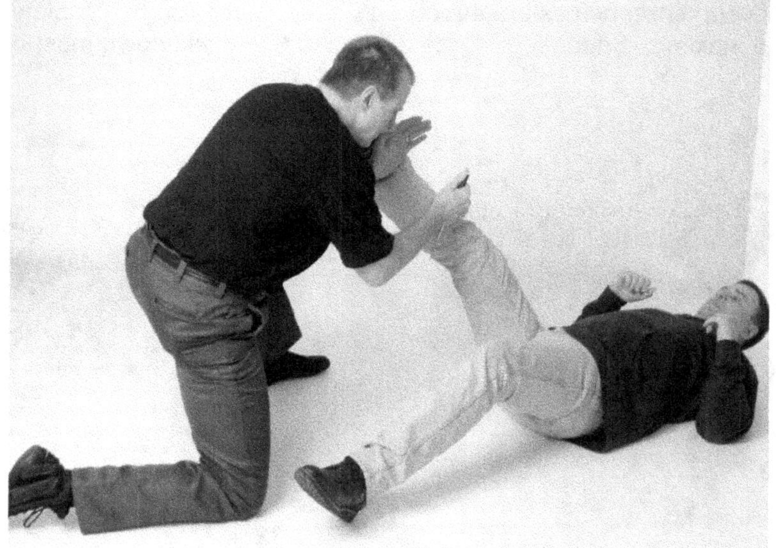

Lower leg.

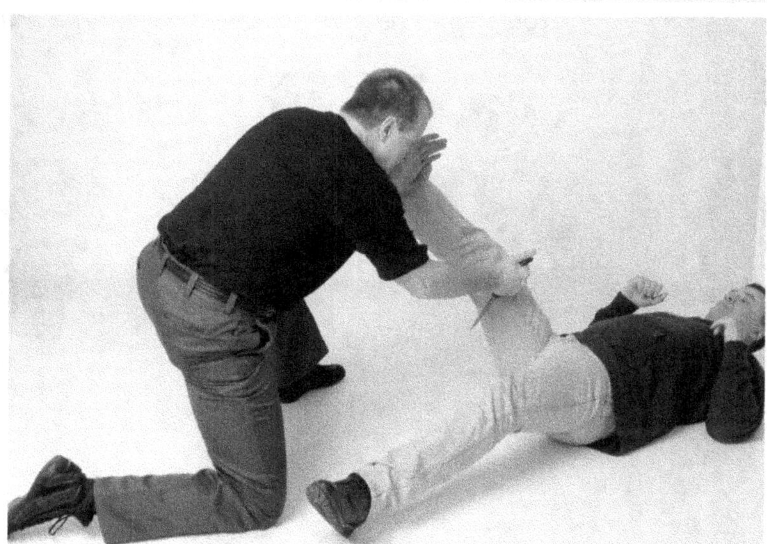

Upper leg.

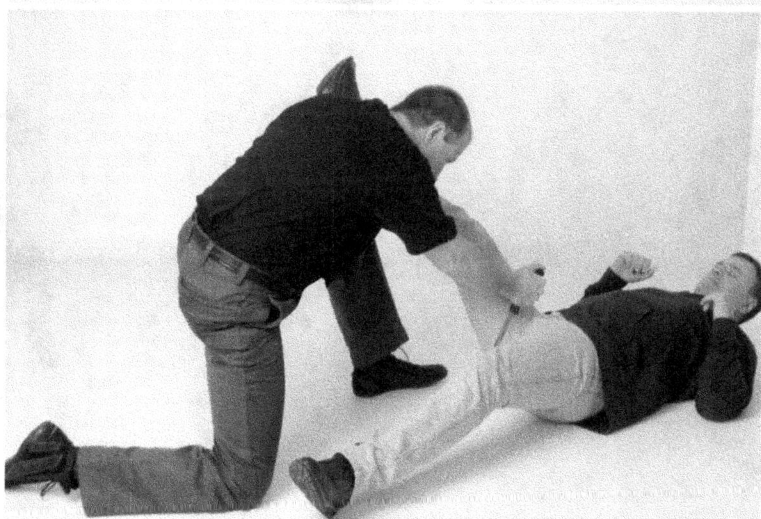

Groin.

Option Awareness Combat Scenario: The Classic Reverse Grip Application

The advanced levels are full of combat scenarios. Here in Level 3 we introduce perhaps the classic, favorite use of the reverse grip. Favored because it demonstrates the hooking and pinching the grip is noted for, of an attacking stab, then the follow-up slash across the throat. This slash must also be considered as an impact strike to the carotid artery to maximize your effect. Once diminished, any takedown must be executed.

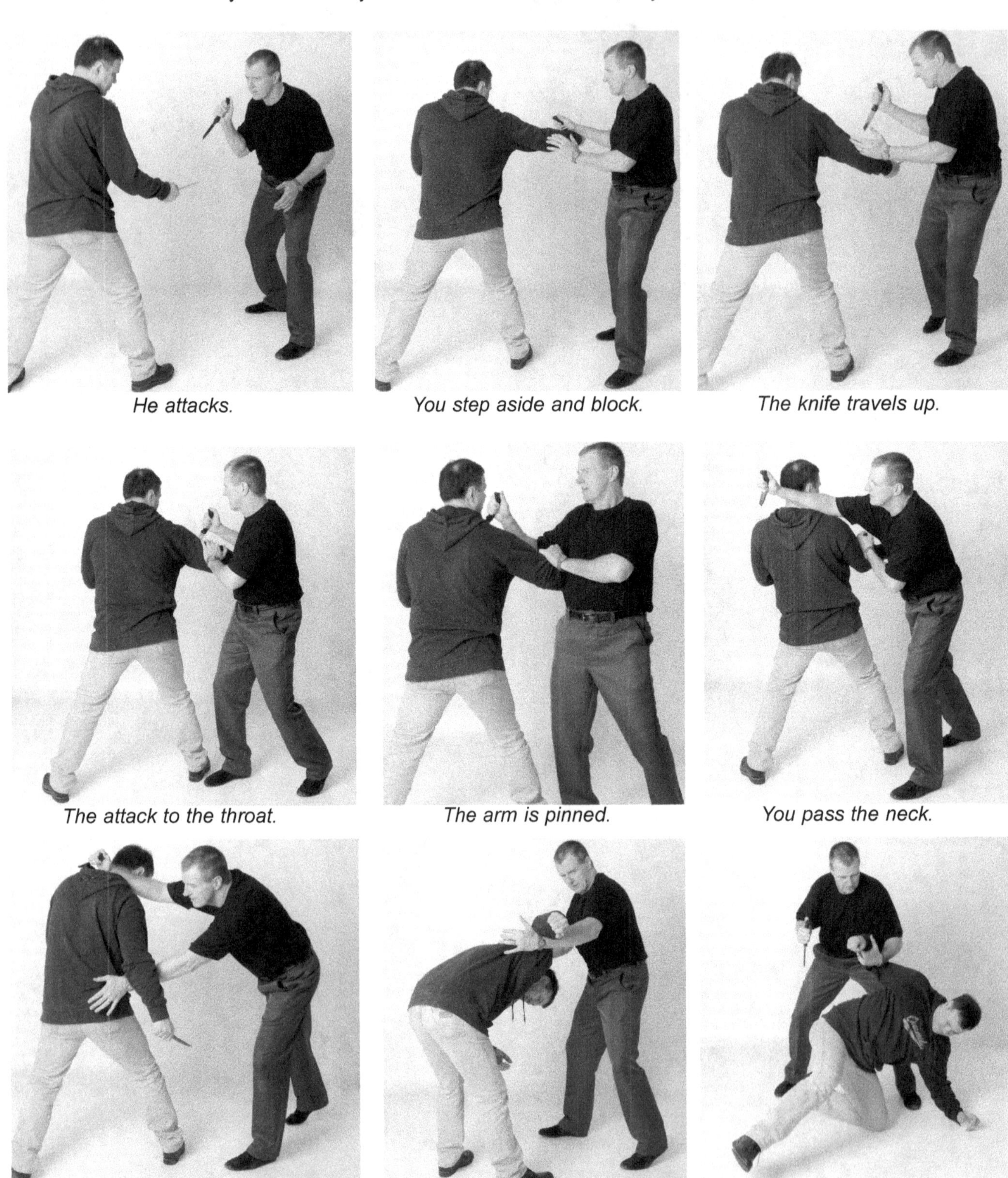

He attacks.

You step aside and block.

The knife travels up.

The attack to the throat.

The arm is pinned.

You pass the neck.

Hook the neck.

Hook the arm.

Spin to a takedown.

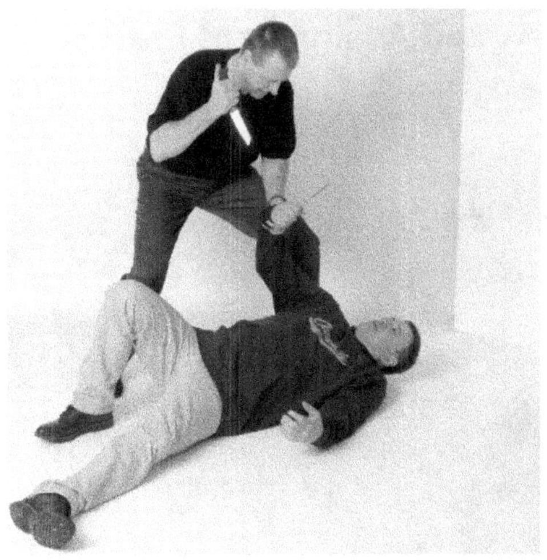 

Finish as needed.

Your Level 3 Knife Workout.

Hit a Training object with:

___ 10 Reverse Grip slashes from 1 o'clock with the right hand.

___ 10 Reverse Grip slashes from 11 o'clock with the left hand.

___ 10 Reverse Grip slashes from the 3 o'clock position.

___ 10 Reverse Grip slashes from the 6 o'clock position.

___ 10 Reverse Grip slashes from the 9 o'clock position.

Block, Pass and Pin Drill

___ Execute half-beat slashes standing trainer.

___ Execute half-beat slashes to a grounded trainer.

Your Knife Reverse Grip Slash Module Review and Assignment Practice

Practice:

The Reverse Slash on the 4 clock quadrants for quick study.

> ___ Standing.
> ___ Walking forward and back.
> ___ Kneeling.
> ___ Ground-on your back.
> ___ Ground-on your side.
> ___ All of the above:
>
>> -on a wooden training "war" post.
>> -on a stick held by a mobile partner.
>> -on animal meat hanging from a post.
>> -with both right and left hands.

The Two Reverse Grip Combination Slashes from the 4 clock quadrants.

> ___ Double slashing (the second slash returns on the same or near line as the first).
> ___ X slashing

Reverse Grip Falling

> ___ Learn to fall forward, backward and to the sides, while holding a saber grip.

Reverse Grip Knee High Drills

> ___ Learn to maneuver knee-high with this drill.

Saber Slash Statue Drill

> ___ Practice the knife-to-arm contact, knife slash method.
> ___ Practice the free hand to arm contact, then knife slash.
> ___ Double arm contact and knife slash.

Practice the Reverse Grip Slash Blocks

> ___ The clock block drills.

Counters to Common Blocks

> ___ Learn to fake (to set up a clear opening).
> ___ Cut the block after contact.
> ___ Re-direct on another line after contact.
> ___ Use the pulling, pinning, passing or pushing of "Invading Hands."

Block, Pass and Pin Skill Drills

    ___ Slash on all the 1/2 beats to develop speed and target acquisition while:
        -standing
        -moving
        -on the ground.

Killshot Knife Sparring

Perform rounds of:

    ___ Right hand versus right hand.
    ___ Left hand versus right hand.
    ___ Left hand versus left hand.
    ___ Short knife versus long knife-any hand.
    ___ Unarmed versus a slasher.

Option Awareness Combat Scenarios

    ___ Practice the *Unarmed Encounters the Slash* scenario.
    ___ Practice the *Street Fighter* knife vs. knife scenario.
    ___ Make a scenario up of your own.

Gun/Counter-Gun
Level 3: Arrest, Control, Restrain and Contain

We've pulled our guns in Level 1. We searched in Level 2. We find him here in Level 3. A citizen, a soldier or an enforcement professional decides what happens next. Do you:

a) Wait for help? Is this plausible?

b) Move in to use ligatures?

c) Prepare for a sudden ambush?
    d) Shoot him?
    e) Search him?

We hope to answer some of these questions and teach you the related tactics in this module.

What's Next?

Studies and Observations 1) Citizen Arrest Issues

Citizens often catch criminals and, at a very base, common law level, initiate legal citizen arrests. However, jurisdiction by jurisdiction, through time, the uncommon laws have become extremely complicated and entwined with numerous lawsuits upon the arresters. Some classes on this subject matter will frighten you into a mindset of inaction.

Ask your local authorities about citizen arrests and subsequent searching. Even in an environment where a citizen can order and have a pizza delivered faster than the response time of a police car, politically correct police officers will always inform you to take no action and await their arrival. Question them further. Even better, consult your local district attorney/prosecutor's office. Juries are often more forgiving to the actions of good samaritans, but in the end a citizen's legal responsibilities usually parallel those of police officers.

There are many lawsuits against citizens and police concerning the loss of freedom on the part of the suspect. When you restrict a suspect's movement by intimidation, threat or physical action you have crossed a legal barrier. You may be responsible for any injuries resulting from the process. If you must take action as a citizen, try to *method-act* like the most professional police officer you can imagine and use only the force necessary to control the enemy. If in realistic fear of your life? Go all out.

> CA 1) Ask your local authorities about citizen arrests and subsequent searching.
> CA 2) Citizen's legal responsibilities parallel police officers.
> CA 3) There are many lawsuits against citizens and police on the:
> -loss of suspect's freedom.
> -injuries resulting from the process.

Always use them because they are statistically very successful. Give very common, simple directional commands. Give them common, simple explanations. Remember simple commands to surrender. Make proclamations that you do not want to hurt them. This might encourage them? It is good for nearby witnesses to hear your wishes.

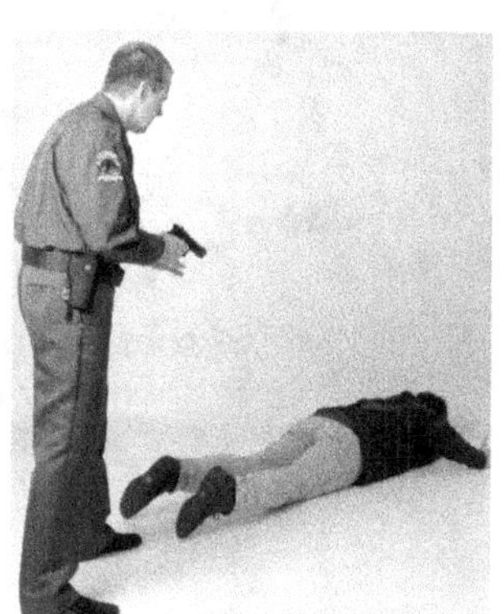

When he is responding, simple, clear verbal commands are statistically successful.

Verbal Commands 1) Always use them (unless it compromises your position in unique circumstances)

    -they are statistically successful.

    -give very common, simple directional commands.

    -give them common, simple explanations.

    -remember simple commands to surrender.

    -make proclamations that you do not want to hurt them.

        *might encourage them?

        *good for nearby witnesses to hear.

Studies and Observations 3) The Basic Arrest Ground Spread Procedure

Police studies have broken down the statistics on who fights their captors and who doesn't. Through the last 10 years, approximately 90 percent of arrested parties comply with the authorities. About 5 percent are passive resistors who do not actively fight back, but physically resist command and physical efforts to secure them. About 4 percent will fight you. Then, the smallest percentage will kill you. Remember these figures relate to law enforcement arrests. Can there can be presumed similarities with military troops taking prisoners or citizen's arrests? Both the military and police command a certain automatic, perceived command presence. If you are just a citizen making a citizen's arrest or interrupting a criminal...results may vary. Should you get your subject to take commands, then:

1) Order him to lie face down.

2) Order him to spread his arms out.

3) Order him to turn his palms upward.

4) Order him to spread his legs.

5) Order him to turn his head away from your direction, and/or cover his head.

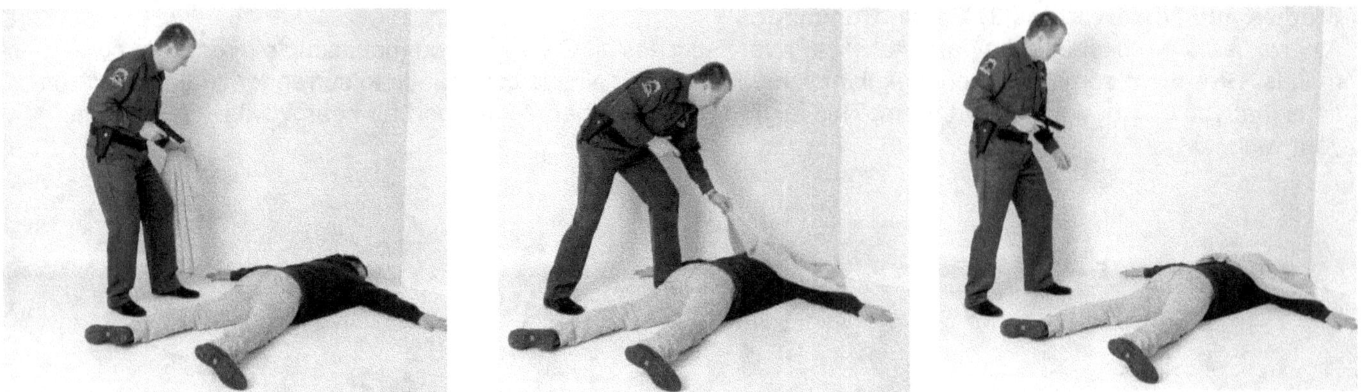

Use something nearby to cover a suspect's head while you perform other vital on-scene tasks or just while waiting for help. He cannot see you to make his escape and counter-attack plans.

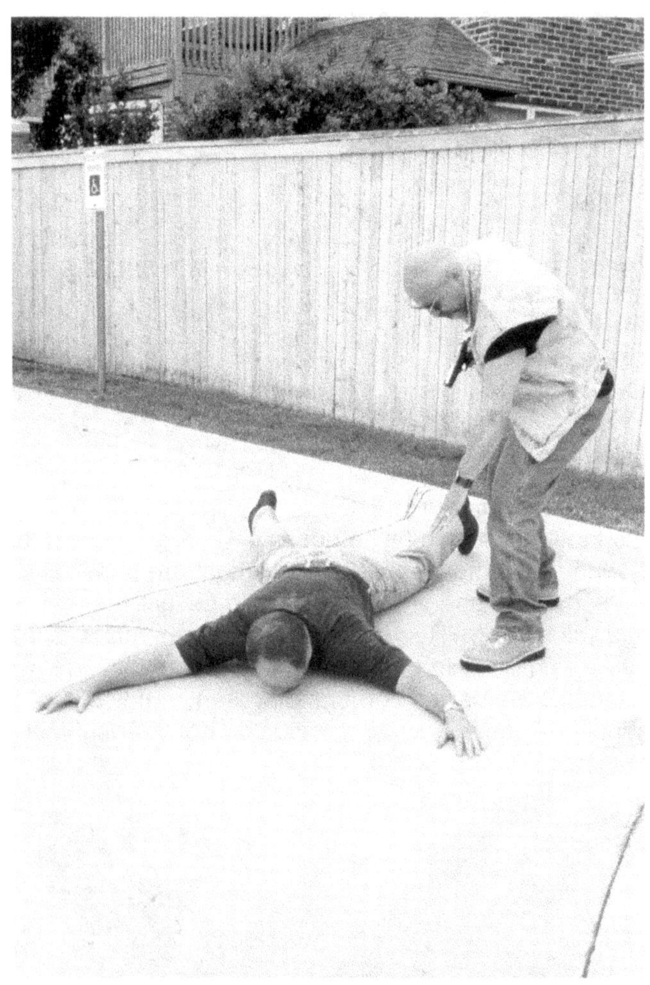

Jerry VanCook, a veteran of hundreds of arrests, many as an undercover narcotics investigator, demonstrates a ground containment. Command presence is a vital part of getting an enemy to respond.

Avoid complacency. A suspect can still get to many of his hidden weapons as he is ordered to a prone position.

Studies and Observations 4) The Custodial Gun Pointing Problem

I have often remarked, "Do you know how many times I have had pistols, shotguns and rifles pointed at me? Hundreds of times! Those of my fellow officers while I am handcuffing or searching a suspect. As we have reviewed extensively in *Training Mission Two*, military and police have muzzling and friendly fire problems.

Look at these two US soldiers teaching indigenous Middle East troops how to effect an arrest. Should that suspect jump, attack or pull a weapon what would the gunman do? Probably, reflexively shoot! And, look at where that long gun is pointed! Look at the distance between the hand of the detainee and the barrel.

The cover operator should position himself in the most advantageous position, while limiting the danger to his partner. This training scenario shows the opposite.

Soldiers are soldiers and police are police. It is hard enough to become graduates of both schools. Teaching a subject you didn't graduate study and complete, is not wise.

Studies and Observations 5) Spray

Spray has a good history in shutting active enemies down. In several studies in the late 1990's and early 2000's, 15 percent to 25 percent of subjects sprayed continued to struggle with officers or were not affected. A key word here is struggle. As a police officer I have sprayed suspects, and in my police spray certification courses, received the mandatory face blasts. Worked on me too, and I know from this negative experience that it is human, reflexive nature to struggle with the results of the blast. Spray itself initiates some level of struggle. You desperately want to cover your eyes, rub your face, etc, all the while officers are trying to restrain you with handcuffs.

Of course you will run across the occasional person who seems unaffected. I prefer and suggest the foamy, stream version rather than the clear, misty spray. The mist will travel in and around you and your target, quickly becoming invisible, while the thick streamer goes where you want, plus you see it and aim it! Later while man-handling the suspect you see where not to touch.

If you can spray paint from a paint can, you can work the tactical spray canister. I ask you to use your spray canister at least once to learn the mechanics of operation. Don't just open the display package and park it on your belt or key chain. And remember to check the expiration dates. Spray is not like wine and does not get better through time.

Basic Use of Force Continuum

Verbal Commands
Physical, unarmed action
Spray
Impact weapons
Firearms

Studies and Observations 6) Handcuffing the Compliant

The methods photographed here have worked millions of times. We'll start with the basic gear.

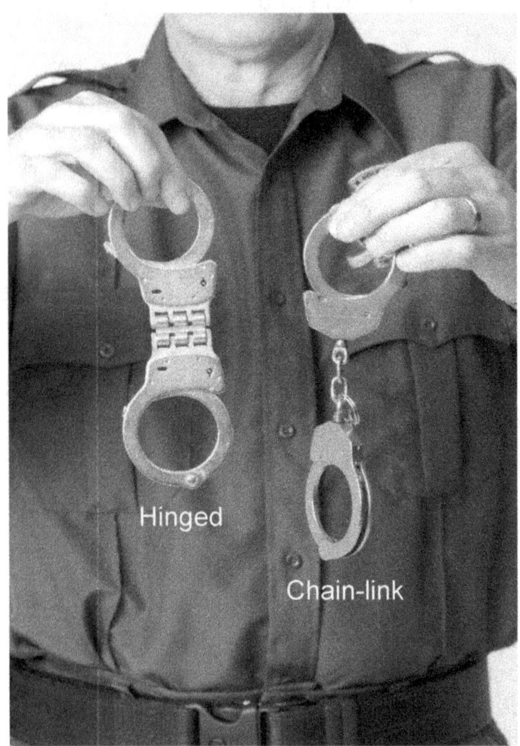

Handcuffs come in two basic packages, hinged (to the far left) and chain-link to the near left and above. The hinged model restricts the suspect's movement. But the limited movement between the bracelets can make it troublesome to handcuff a opponent during a fight. The chain link may be easier to apply, but will allow the suspect to move his hands more than with hinges.

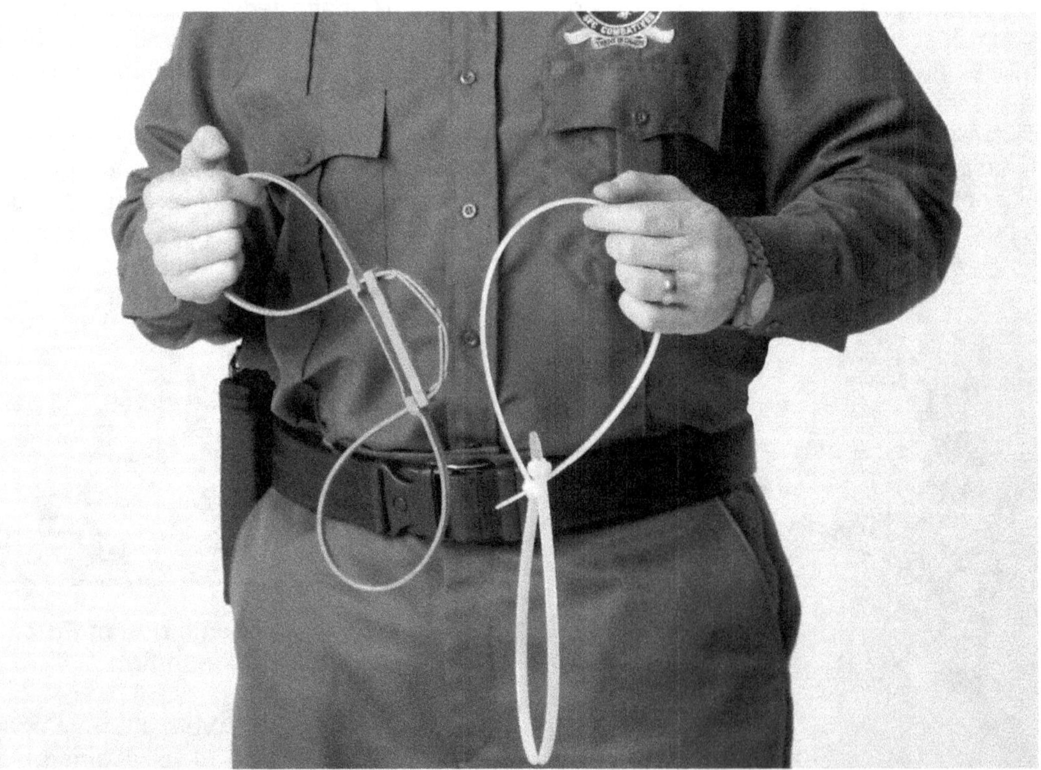

Plastic flexi-cuffs are lighter and easier to carry (even the 1970's we asked for wire wraps from telephone company repairmen, storing them inside our hats) Now they are professionally made and designed for law enforcement, but civilians can buy the originals at hardware store. Remember these may be used as ankle/leg hobbles.

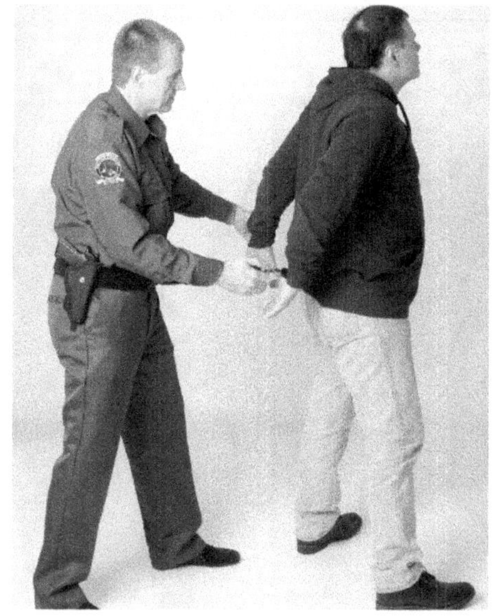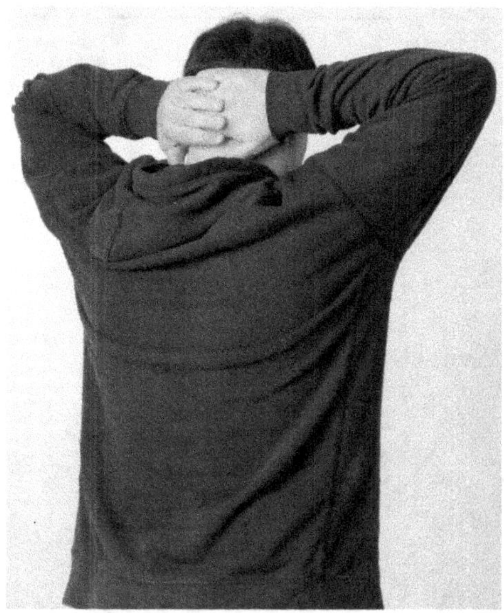

Common positions that professionals order compliant subjects into for restraints are:

1) Arms down.
2) Hands behind the neck or atop the head.
3) Arms spread out.
4) Standing
5) Kneeling
6) Prone

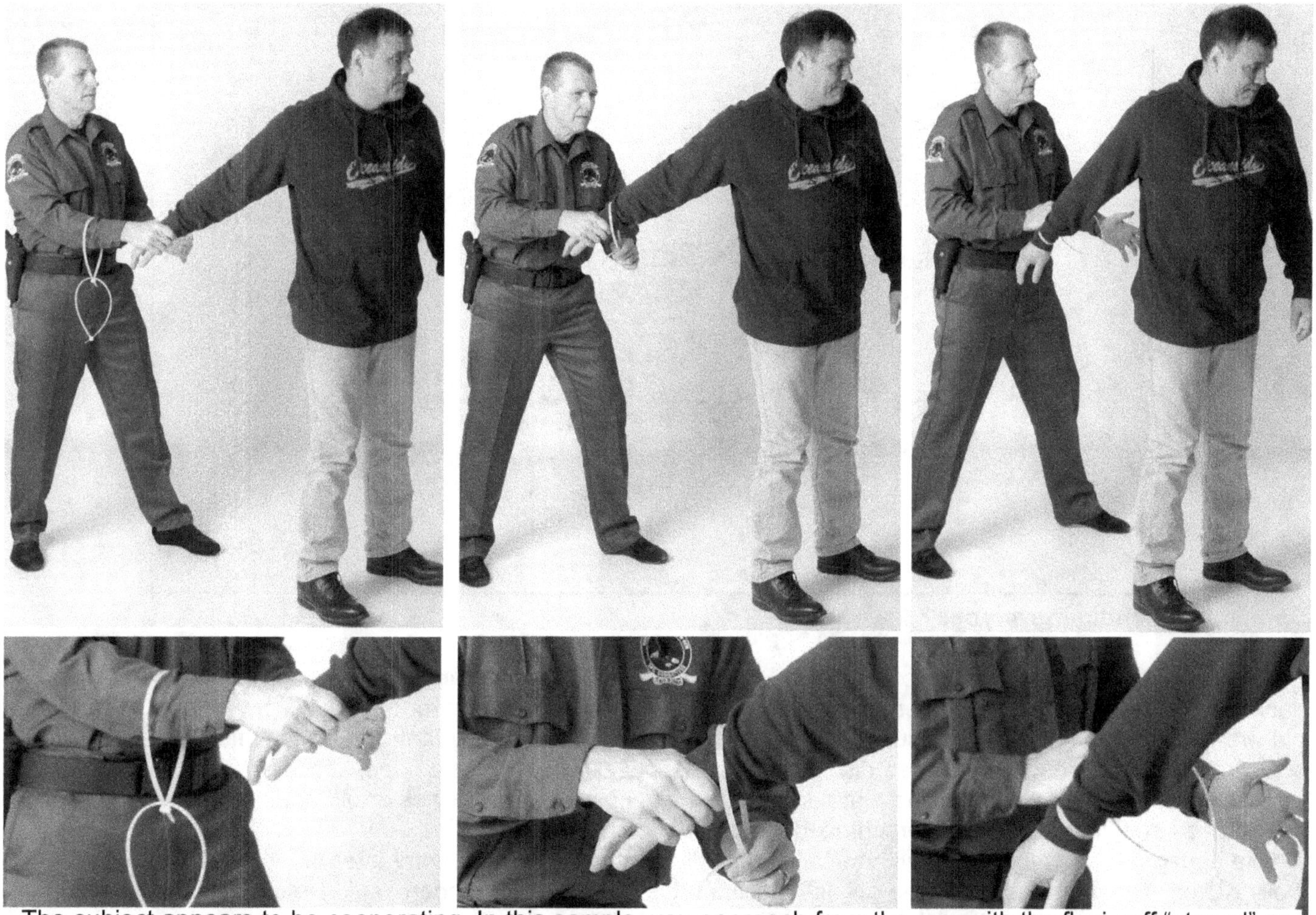

The subject appears to be cooperating. In this sample, you approach from the rear with the flexi-cuff "staged"-as in looped on your arm. You grip the compliant arm, then slip the loop up on the captured wrist. Pull it tight. Then order the delivery of the second hand, or reach, grab and pull the second hand over to the free loop of the flexi-cuff. Hook it and pull.

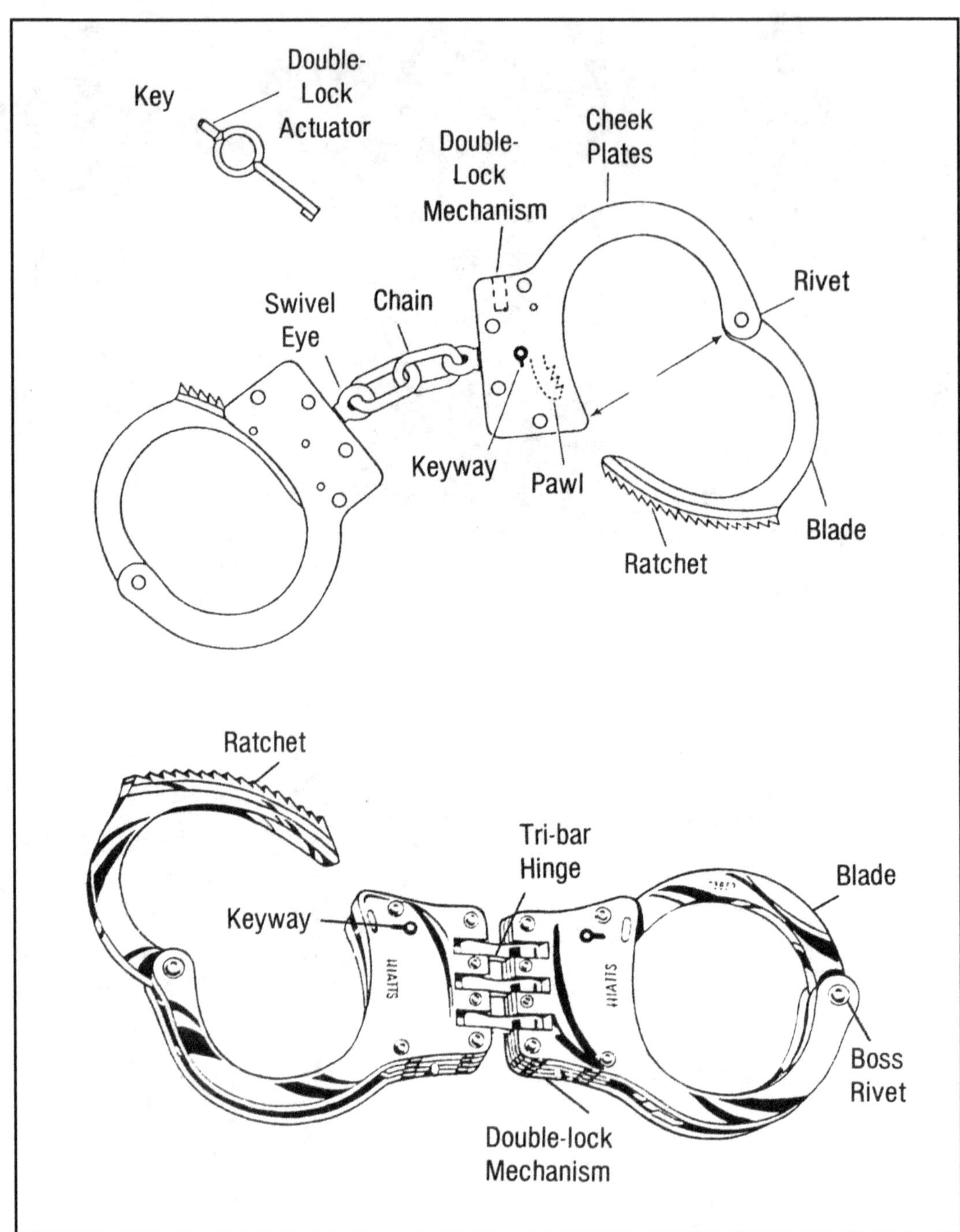

Should you handcuff everyone? Always?

Ask the officers in Highland Park, TX. Police guidelines there calling for anyone wanted on a warrant to be handcuffed while arrested have been revamped following the public outcry over an officer's arrest of a 97-year-old woman. The woman was handcuffed and taken to jail for an outstanding traffic warrant. Officers in the Dallas suburb of Highland Park now can use discretion in arrest cases if they have a supervisor's approval. Several factors will be weighed when making that decision, including physical disabilities or old age. The same criteria will be used in determining if the person needs to be handcuffed.

The department was inundated with e-mails and calls from around the country after the April 22 arrest of Dolly Kelton. The revisions clarify the options officers have in arresting offenders, said Detective Randy Millican, public information officer for the Highland Park Department of Public Safety. "I think it's appropriate to say we have defined some discretionary areas without placing at risk our officers," he said.

The Classic Standing Handcuff Process for the Compliant

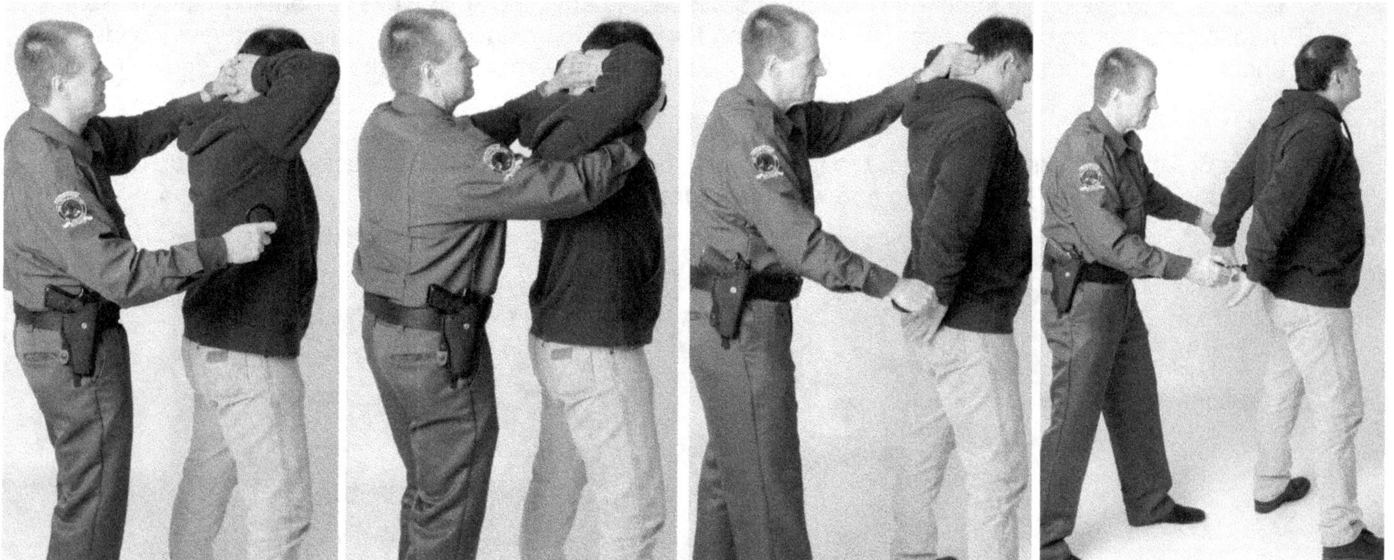

One method of many: He complies. You thread the right arm. Cuff and pull down. Get the other arm.

More issues in handcuffing:
There are week-long classes on this subjects and the variations of positions and tactics. Imagine the combinations and possibilities.

Issue 1: Citizens and metal handcuffs.
Should law enforcement find you with handcuffs, they will suspect you of using them as a sexual toy OR, an implement of a serial killer. Be prepared to answer questions.

Issue 2: The term "tactical handcuffing."
This is a term used by law enforcement professionals when teaching classes on the subject. All the material therein is tactical in nature.

Issue 3: What is the leading edged-weapon injury to law enforcement?
The open end of an officer's handcuff, flying loose when trying to arrest a non-complying subject, is classified as the leading edged-weapon injury.

Issue 4: Perfect world positioning of cuffs for maximum efficiency.
When you know you are going to use them, the hand holds the bracelet in the ready-to-strap-on position. Technicians suggest you "load" them in such a manner that the last tooth/click is in gear.

Issue 5: The speed cuffing myth
There have been many self-proclaimed experts, some of them martial artists, inventing elaborate and ridiculous cuffing moves against choreographed suspects. These maneuvers dazzle the naive and insult the veteran's sensibilities. In the end, simple is best. With this simplicity comes speed. With smoothness comes speed.

Issue 6: Cuffs too tight? Everyone's complaint!
Suspects will continue to whine about the tightness of the cuffs. At times they will push the bracelets tighter as they sit. There are indeed some medical problems that can occur. If you double lock the cuffs the teeth will lock in place. There are police agencies that require such double-locking, and mandate the step be recorded in the arrest paperwork. As a result, many handcuffing instructors dictate that the double-lock hole and key hole be on the topside and easily accessibly. But, the ease of subsequent unlocking is really is too much to worry about in the field. Sort it all out in the jail room book-in!

Issue 7: Beware cuffing your suspect to other items.
Decades ago, we could temporarily handcuff a suspect to anything solid while performing other tasks. In today's law enforcement, this is frowned upon for fear of injury lawsuits. I would not outlaw the idea under certain circumstances. Citizens and the military may use this tactic without restrictive guidelines.

Issue 8: Three across trick for big, broad suspects, or for non-complying suspects resisting you with arms locked in isometrically. Bridge the gap with that extra set.

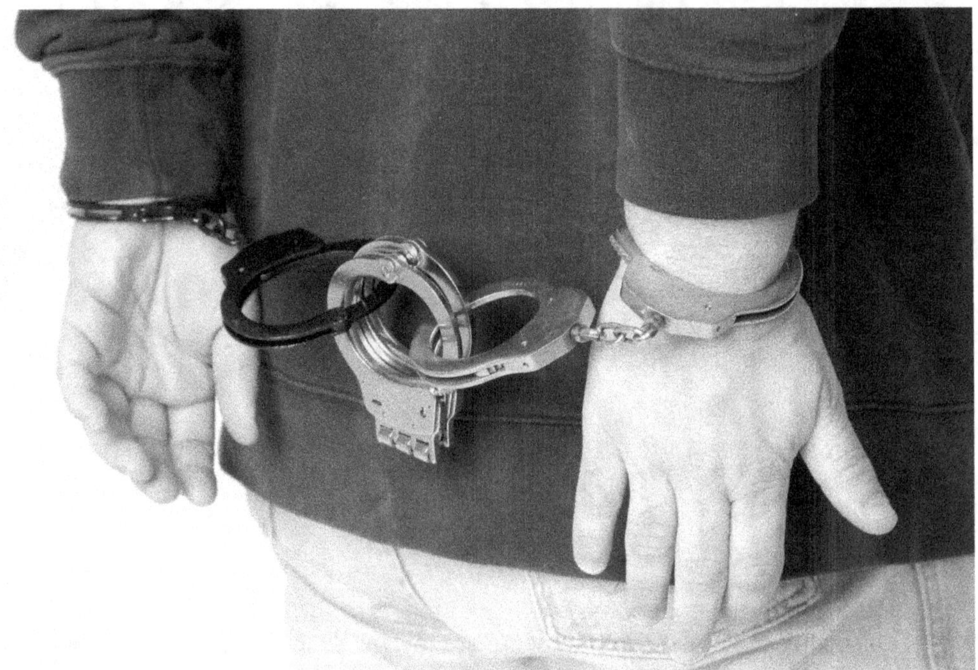

Three across trick for big, broad suspects, or for non-complying suspects resisting you with arms locked in isometrically. Bridge the gap with that extra set.

Issue 9: Self-cuffing kidnap escape trick
Often, criminals hold weapons on officers and order the officer to handcuff themselves. If it comes to this? Teach yourself this trick. Learn how to feed the teeth OUTSIDE the bracelet while clicking a few teeth through the free end. This makes the sound of secured cuff. Make sure the bent-over ratchet is on the bottom side. Then really handcuff your other wrist in the other side. At the first opportune moment, free yourself and attack.

Issue 10: Right hand first
Statistics tell us that most people are right-handed. Confine that stronger, more coordinated side first.

Issue 11: Other ligatures like wires, rope, drapes... anything.
There are legal issues surrounding any ligature use applied on a person. Threats and lawsuits of false arrest, kidnapping and false imprisonment may arise. Always consult your local authorities. When trying to constrain an enemy, use the handy items around you. Experiment with a dress belt and a training partner. Think about the electric wire found in almost every room. Duck tape has thousands of uses and one is for binding up suspects. Figure four style wraps work well. You should crunch the tape where possible. A unwatched suspect may find a sharp corner and cut through the tape. Remember this trick if you are kidnapped. Another escape trick! While you are being bound up by rope, tighten all your muscles and expand your body in every way. Later, when left alone, you might be able to slip through your bonds.

Studies and Observation 7) Ground, Rear/Saddle Handcuffing the Compliant

The opponent complies (or is forced faced down). Another pass-thru step from the standing to ground position is the rear saddle, one that is self-explanatory. Hook the arm into the rear arm bar position. Clamp this bent arm in with your thigh. Get the hand/wrist into the small of the back. Place your thighs up against his elbow and forearm to restrict his movement.

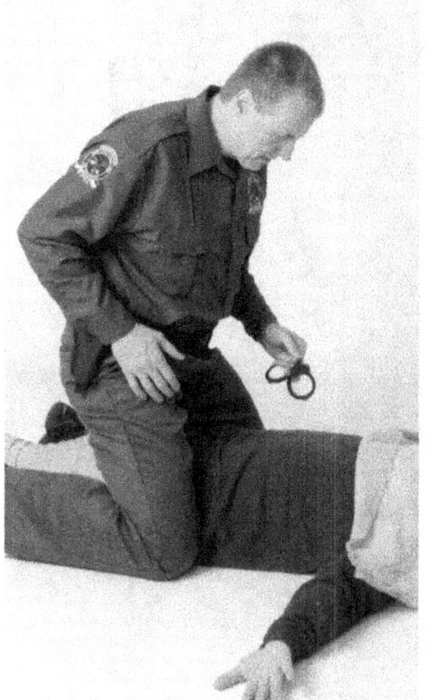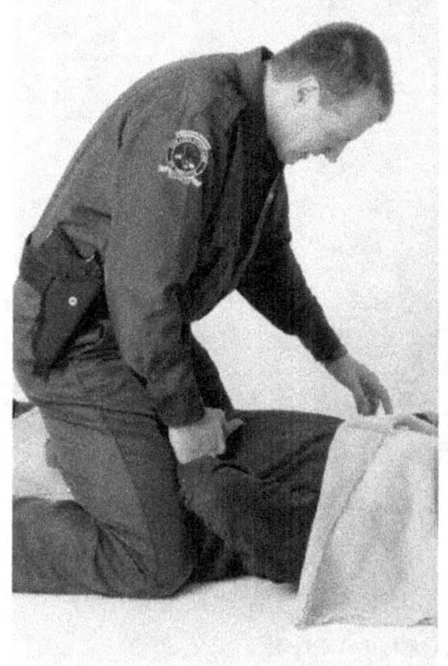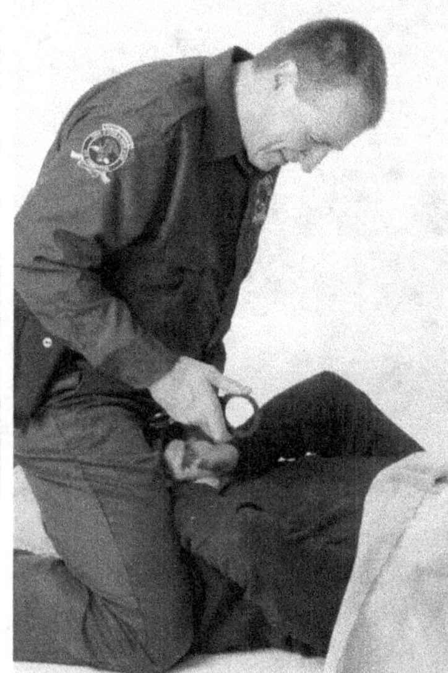

Rear saddle. Grab and pull an arm to the rear. Get the other arm. Use your thighs to force the arms into position.

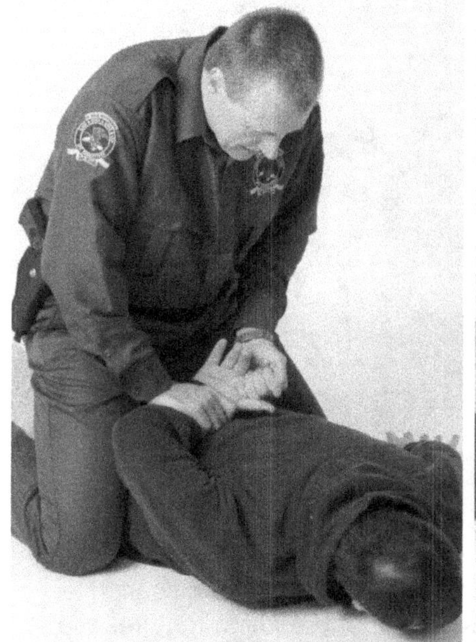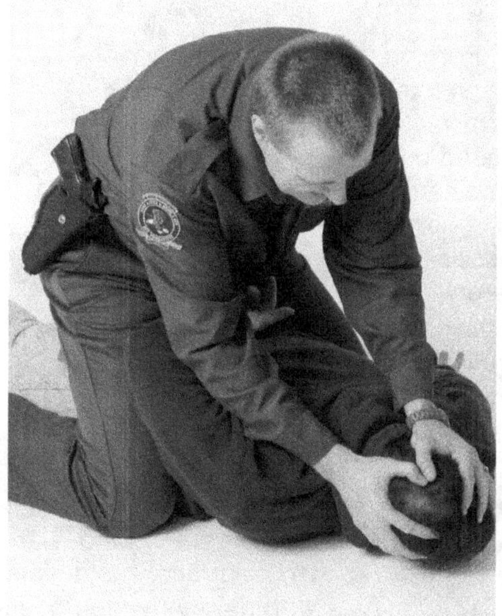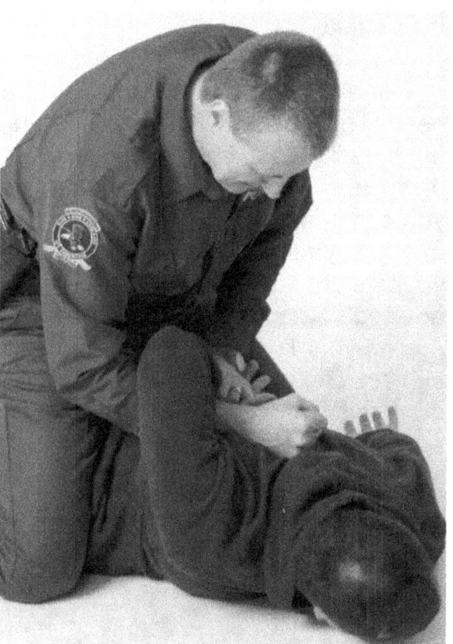

Crank the fingers to get compliance, or....rake the head across the ground.   *Or, crank the arm back.*

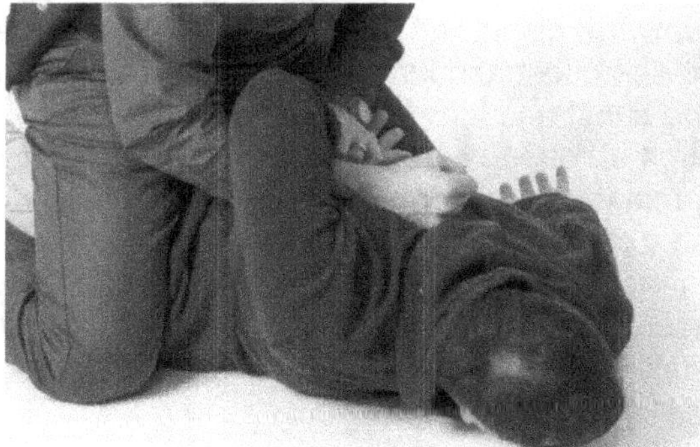

If he suddenly refuses your commands to place his other arm into ligature capture position, you can apply several tactics, all the while giving him verbal commands.

To get this painful arm crank, insert your arm into the bend of his caught arm, bottom-side entry. Put your fist across the spinal cord onto the far shoulder blade, or as far as you can naturally reach. Raise your arm and lean your body across the back for pain compliance.

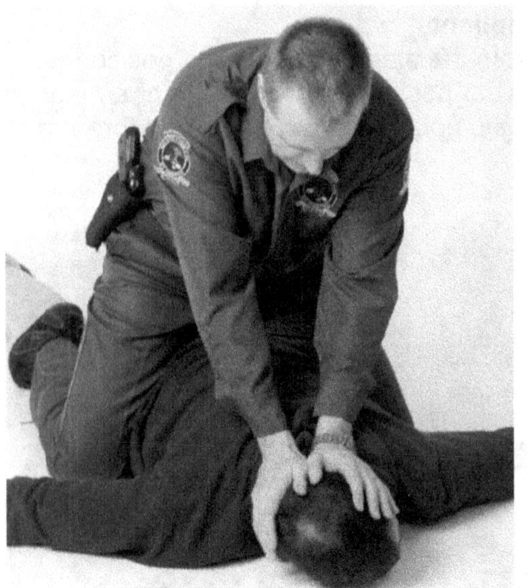
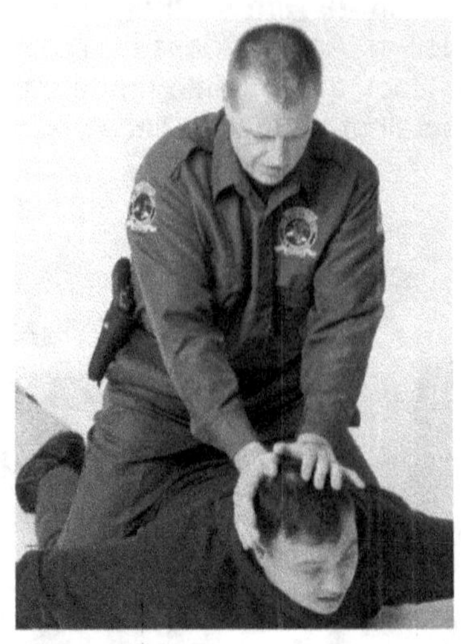

Push the head down, causing the head to raise and resist. Let it.   *Then, slip your arm into the new opening.*

Most law enforcement is forbidden to choke, or so much as touch anyone's throat. Even if they are fighting for their life, such action will be weighed very heavily against them. But civilians and the military have much more leeway when fighting for their safety.

Open a path for a choke by pushing down on the head. This almost always causes the person to push back. Let it raise, then slip your arm into this newly acquired space. Manipulate the head until you can squeeze the windpipe and/or the carotid. Interlock your hand into your forearm. Dropping your weight squarely on his back will assist. Be advised you could kill him! Also take care when putting your knee into the chest or the back of a subject. Depending upon the health condition of the man, this might incite a deadly condition called positional asphyxia.

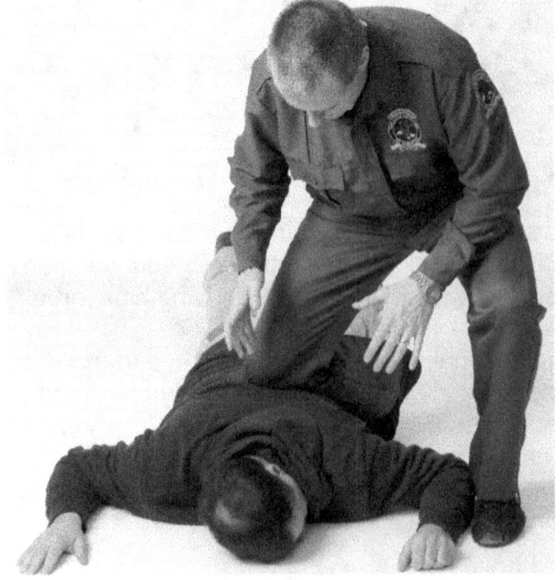

Michael P. Stone is an attorney in Pasadena, CA, USA, whose practice is devoted to defending police officers. He warns, " everyone understands that breathing requires the inhalation of oxygen-laden air. In order to expand the chest and lungs to accommodate the air coming in, the diaphragm moves downward, displacing for a second or two, the abdominal viscera. The chest and lungs are then permitted to expand.

Now, if the chest and lung area cannot expand sufficiently to pull in enough air due to external weight, force and pressure, the person may be on his or her way to dying."

With each exhalation, the force and weight compresses the space even more. Panic-stricken, the subject may thrash around, causing even more restraint action and even more pressure. This is the so-called "python-effect." Cardiac arrest follows quickly.

Leg and Bent Knee Ground Captures

The grounded position is a common step for approaching and cuffing your grounded subject. If you have to approach him, one method is through leg control measures.

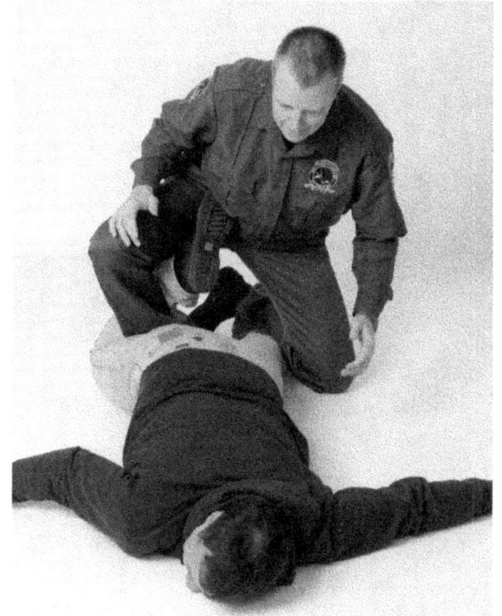

Single leg lock (and shin trap).

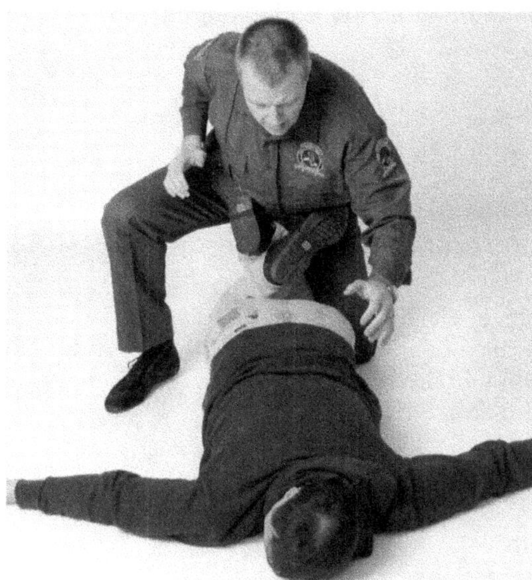

Double leg lock.

Watch out for a push back!

These leg locks are frequently taught, but when applied against a strong or excited person, great kick back power can be exerted through his legs, tossing you backwards. At times, rollovers are also possible. Watch out for a guy tucking his arm and shoulder under his chest. With a little pain tolerance on his part, he may roll over and escape. The leg locks have to be executed impeccably, which also includes quickly. The quicker you can create a tight bend, the less strength he can muster.

The Shin Rake

When sufficient help has arrived and your subject has locked himself into a non-cooperative isometric position, step to the rear. Your comrades are topside. Feed a stick under his leg and grab it into a "X" grip. Now start raking the shin up and down. This causes excruciating pain. Command him to put his hands to his back.

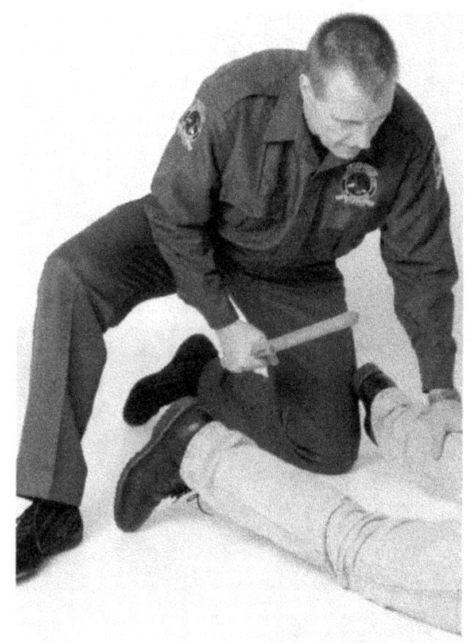

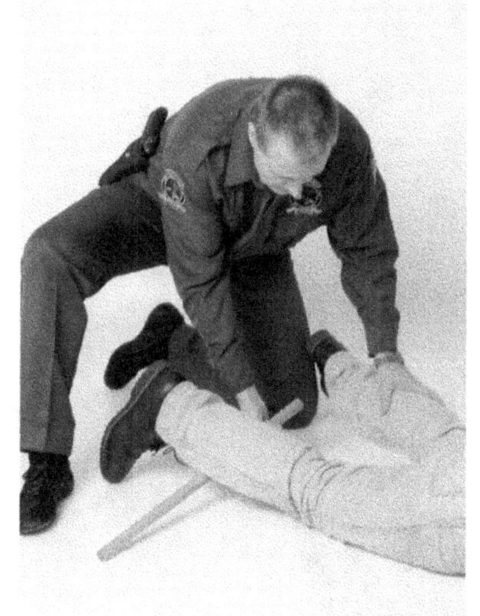

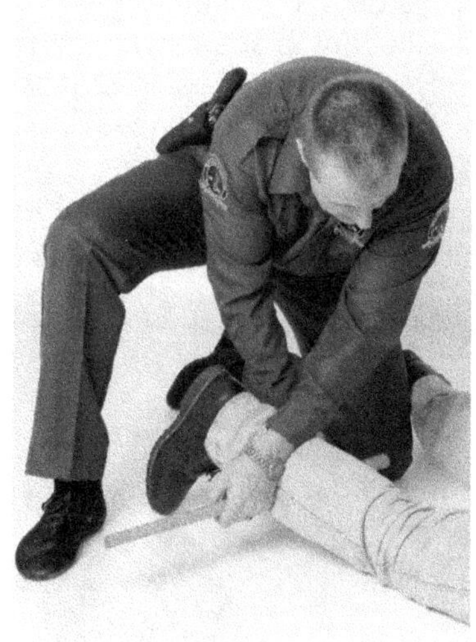

Not cooperating? Insert the stick under his leg. Grab the stick in a double-hand "X." Start raking up and down.

Tip Offs He May Attack

When a person becomes stressed, his body undergoes a series of
physiological changes. Here are some changes that research,
history and experience may be linked to a sudden attack upon you.

Head

His eyes bulge.
He has that 1000 yard stare.
He ignores you.
He squints.
He assesses your body parts and gear as potential targets.
His mouth becomes dry.
His teeth clench.
His voice changes.
He actually clearly voices violent intentions.
His words become spastic and distracted.
He twitches.
His nostrils flare.
His breathing increases
He takes one big sudden breath.
His face color changes, maybe reddens or pales.
His veins bulge.
His chin tightens, or drops.
His neck tightens.

Hands and Arms

His fingers and fists clench (blood leaving the extremities).
His fingers drum surface tops.
His hands shake.
His hands and arms travel to pre-fight positions:
      -near possible weapons on or near him
      -raises up to seemingly innocent, high positions as in
       a fake head scratch, a yawn or a stretch.

Body

He raises from seated positions.
He tries to wander.
He gets to close.
His body blades away from you.
He takes off his shirt or jacket.
He bends at the knees.
Heel and toe tapping.
Positioning near potential weapons.
Positions himself very near you.

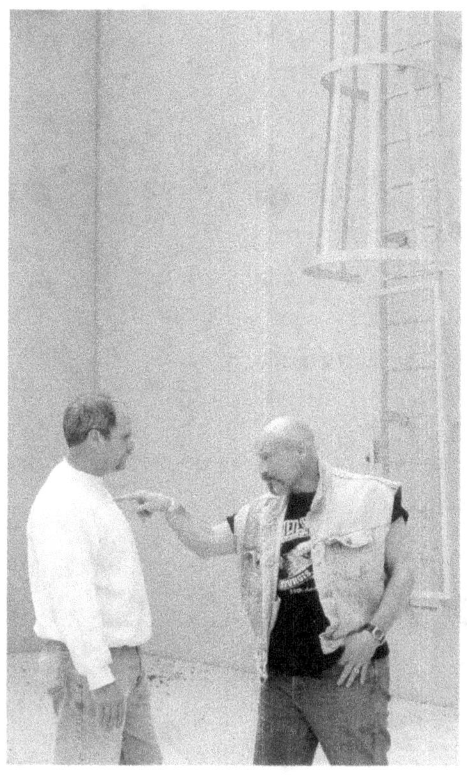

Whether detaining a possible criminal or an enemy soldier, always try to maintain enough space between the two of you to assess the situation. To the left, Barnhart allows VanCook in way too close. Above,. Barnhart allows himself some reaction space and time. The key test question to see if your command presence is working? When you order the individual to turn around. Turn around, or possibly order, "get down on your knees," also the first step for many authorities in the detainment process, will help establish his level of cooperation and then the rest of your plan.

Unsure he's your guy? You may not be able to draw down on him, but rather, you may try to engage in conversation from a safe distance. How he reacts to you will tip you off as to whether you need to escalate or de-escalate.

This is one of my favorite interview stances, I have taught it at police academies since the 1980s. My arms are positioned such that they will not be pinned if charged. I can strike with the lead arm and draw a weapon with the rear.

The Chase Drill

He suddenly turns and runs! Your adrenaline erupts like a volcano and you are in the classic foot pursuit. If you're a cop you can barely report this on your portable radio between desperate breaths. If you're a soldier, you might shout to your team. If you're a citizen dedicated to stopping a criminal, you probably are alone! Then...he turns back on you! What's in his hand now? Is that a set of keys? A gun? Do you draw and shoot? Is he surrendering, or trying to kill you?

This is an all-to-common incident in the world of fighting crime and terrorism. I have created this drill to enhance skills and promote vital, simulated training experience. It must be run with simulated ammo and appropriate safety gear. I prefer the battery-powered, so-called "electric guns," because the pellet flies true with only a slight sting. The runner needs a series of props in his pocket such as a pistol, a badge, keys, etc., to pull out, turn and surprise your trainee.

1) Hock starts the run. Jeff "Rawhide" Laun waits 5 seconds, then chases.

2) Then Hock stops suddenly, turns...

3) ...and surrenders. Rawhide stops and stands ready.

4) Rawhide initiates his arrest, control and contain skills.

1) Another chase starts.

2) Hock turns on the run...

3)...and it's a moving gunfight!

Remember you will be chasing people inside and outside buildings, and in all kinds of urban, rural and suburban terrain. Combat is situational. The alley to the left offers potential for cover. Practice for all kinds of situations. Less time on the range. More sims! More sims! MORE SIMS!

Photos by Bill Whitworth

Studies and Observations 8: Is He Dead Yet?

At times when a citizen or a police officer shoots a criminal, or when soldiers shoot the enemy in the chaos of battle, they may find it difficult to determine the precise results of their gunfire. They must make a quick decision whether the subject is dead, in order to proceed with their mission. To advance or search for other suspects, or safely secure the ones you have downed, you will need to approach the body. Many searchers have been surprised or shot by a suspect faking death. Many have been shot or stabbed in the back after passing a downed subject.

Here are some of the methods used to successfully accomplish this evaluation. Also, please take note that many of these rules may also apply to the detection of subjects who have been knocked unconscious.

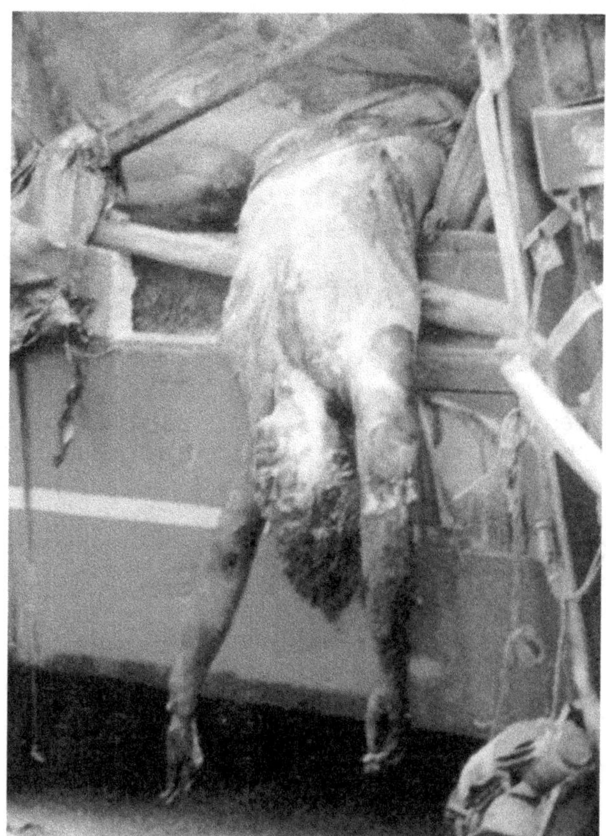

If a person assumes a position that looks difficult if not impossible to maintain for very long, it's increasingly likely the suspect is dead.

The "Get-Up" Position
If a person faked death and planned to ambush you, you might see him in some sort of quick get-up position so he might attack you. His hands might lay palms down and he may be foolish enough to lay almost in a push-up, exercise position. He might place his legs and feet in such a manner as to suggest a quick leap to his feet. He might pick his position on these grounds.

The Drilled
From a distance, examine the subject. Usually a powerful bullet, which lands on either side of the center a person, and causes a quick kill, will create a drilling effect. The person will "spin" or drill downward in a loose spiral. This process will often cause the feet and ankles to interlock when he comes to rest.

The Fallen Marionette
Does the body have the look of a marionette-puppet whose strings have suddenly been cut? If your rounds caused a quick kill, the body will usually fall in complete disarray.

The Painful Posture
If the wounded person died in much pain, and not from a quick kill, the two elements above may not describe what you find. Instead, hands may have clutched body parts. In longer term developing death situations, soldiers report approaching bodies that have mementos like wallet photos scattered near, as though the person experienced nostalgia before his death, all clues.

Defecation and Urination
Many times as you approach the body you may detect the smell of, or spy the stains of feces or urine; when the body dies, many muscles relax. If the person *evacuated* prior to the combat he would have nothing to lose. It is always wise to empty his bowels and bladder before danger because of the strong statistical possibility that a lower torso wound might clip your intestines and poison your insides.

An Obvious Devastating Wound
It can be visually apparent upon your approach that a significant wound has killed your enemy. Sometimes a large quantity of blood may be present, an amount that would suggest death.

Long Term Miscellaneous Clues
The presence of fly swarms and/or maggots or the mouth and nose submerged in puddles or ponds for a period of observation, longer than a few minutes, may also be a definitive clue to the condition of the body. There is also a distinct smell.

Booby-Trapped
Be cautious of explosives planted on bodies triggered to detonate upon investigation of the body. In our militant times, citizens and police must also consider such possibilities, not just our soldiers! Rigging a long-range device with sticks or ropes may allow you to hook and manipulate the body from a safe range.

Throwing Objects
One test is to throw some objects at the body to check for reaction.

Approach with Caution
Approach with gun up and caution. Prepare for a surprise. Can you see both hands? Where might he reach for a gun or a knife? Under his torso? Concealed nearby? In the military, a downed person is used as bait for an enemy sniper. Act according to the circumstances.

Final Death Throes
The human body may still quiver and move shortly after death. Seeing a spastic jolt may not be a clue that the subject is alive and waiting to jump you.   Such spasms may cause additional fire into a "deceased person" which, under the circumstances of present witnesses may look excessive.

The "Eyes Have It" The Final Test
Some vets have reported looking at the open eyes of their subject, trying to detect a blink as they approached. The many military personnel have unofficially developed the "eye thump" test. A finger thump to the eyeball is a telltale that the person's nervous system has shut down.

Summary Examination
. Are the ankles interlocked?
. Is the configuration disarrayed?
. Is it a painful posture?
. Is he in any kind of "get-up" position?
. Are there signs of defecation and urination?
. Is there an obvious, devastating wound?
. Beware of booby traps.

Suggested Action
. Throw objects.
. Use tools to probe suspicious bodies from a distance.
. Approach your downed targets with caution.
. Use the eye thump test.

Regardless of your discovery, your department and/or unit procedures may require you to apply ligatures to the body as a matter of routine before continuing on with your work. There are of course those dangerous times in hot lines of fire when you cannot tiptoe up to each subject Also, please remember this information because someday you may be in a position when **_you_** must surprise your approaching enemy. Remember these rules to create a successful trap.

Steve Krystek of Vegas Metro trains for a surprise knife quick draw of a suspect.

You've got him?

Or you thought you had! During the process he has bucked up on you. He has pulled a weapon, charged you, or started his run all over again. Whether you are a civilian stopping the escape of a criminal, a soldier or a cop, here are some tips that might help you defeat someone who falsely surrenders.

Pulling Weapons! Watch the hands! It's the hands that will kill you.
A subject routinely puts his hands up to show surrender-almost an instinctive move-baring the palms of his hands. But as you well know, his hands up mean they are near a combat ready position to attack you. Watch the hands! It's the hand that will kill you. Always be aware that his hands may be traveling to a carry site on his body.

The common two-hand surrender pose.

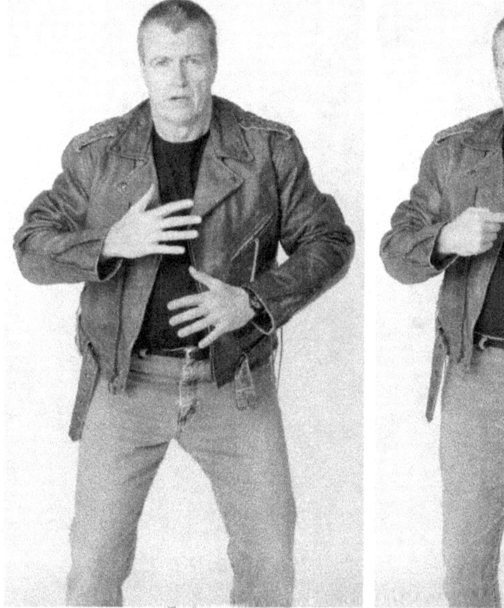

The "Who? Me?" surprise pose. But, he really puts his hand near...a shoulder holster.

Weapon Detection! Is your subject armed? In ***Training Mission One*** we documented the carry sites of weapons. Review this material. Look at the primary, secondary and tertiary carry sites of your subject. You will be trying to detect a variety of belt-line and armpit carries, pocket carries, holsters and then off-the body hiding spots within his lunge and reach.

<table>
<tr><td>

Weapon Detection Tips

WD 1) Review carry sites.
WD 2) Recognize concealment clothing and weapon, clothing prints.
WD 3) Recognize body adjusting and uncomfortable body movements identified with gun carrying.
WD 4) Recognize nearby, lunge and reach sites where he can grasp a weapon.

</td></tr>
</table>

A strange surrender pose. His one hand is near a belt line holster.

Memorize these common gun and knife drawing hand motions. React when you see them.

The cross-over quick draws. High into the armpit. Low on the belt line.

Itchy forearm? No! A forearm sheath and knife.

Beware this move. Many guns and knives are carried center-chest.

Tom Barnhart reaches for a backpack weapon from
a common hands up position. He also goes for
his boot knife when ordered prone.

Imagine the possibilities to conceal a weapon quick draw from a car.

Beware of the Turn-Around Trick

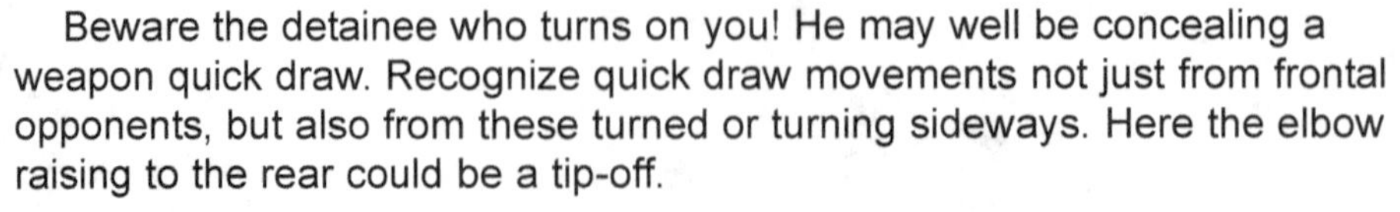

Beware the detainee who turns on you! He may well be concealing a weapon quick draw. Recognize quick draw movements not just from frontal opponents, but also from these turned or turning sideways. Here the elbow raising to the rear could be a tip-off.

Also identify the sounds of folding knives clicking opening. Listen for the sounds when in the field. A common attacker here would thrust his left hand into your face, charge and stab your torso with his knife.

Statistics say most people are right-handed. It would be common for people to turn to their right side to access a concealed weapon.

Whether pulling a knife or a gun from your belt line, the motions of the shoulder, elbow, wrist and hand are much the same. The steps and so much more have been chronicled in **_Training Mission One._**

Beware of Flying Objects

Anything in the hands of someone you confront might convert into a makeshift weapon or an object tossed at you for just an instant's distraction, long enough to get part of a quick draw process underway.

Legendary FBI Agent Delf Bryce, veteran of scores of combat shoot-outs.

Quite a few old FBI agents were amazing quick draw shootists and proved their skills in combat, like Delf Bryce shown to the left, many times. In an era of fast shooting gangsters, they had too. In an off-air conversation with G. Gordon Liddy, himself a former agent and agency quick draw record holder, The G-Man told me that one of their FBI Academy tactics was to look as if they were scratching their head or shifting back their standard issue fedora hats on their heads. Then they would suddenly toss their hat at an opponent and quickly draw their service revolver. They practiced this hat toss on the range.

An old veteran Chicago, IL. street cop and detective of the 1950s and 1960s, encouraged our police class to throw anything handy at a potential gun man for a distraction. He told us,

"Do anything to get the upper hand on a thug. This game's for keeps!"

Beware the Static Line Weapon

Innocent enough looking, there may well be a weapon hooked to the other end of any cord. You spot it and he reaches into the pocket and grabs the handle of the knife. He pulls. The shorter the cord, the shorter the time before the sheath stops and the knife is out. There are small pistols built on the same types of rigs.

Be on the look-out for the static line like this. There could be a knife at the other end.

Look at the action. The sheath stays, the knife is exposed.

Beware of the Offered Pistol

When I started in police work in the 1970s, revolvers were the weapons of choice for the law officer. As an Army investigator I was even issued a Snub nose .38 revolver, but as a military patrolman in the U.S. and South Korea they issued me the classic 1911, .45 semi-auto, which I preferred for all the obvious, tactical reasons. In 1977, I began working in a Texas department where semi-autos were outlawed and actually nicknamed "newfangled" and I heard them called "Buck Roger's guns," by a crusty old-timer, who actually carried a pearl-handled pistol that suspiciously resembled something Gene Autrey had worn in a black and white western. It is hard to remember those old days when both the good guys and the bad guys almost exclusively carried wheel guns.

Back then, I was taught a series of revolver tricks by veteran and retired FBI agents that may not see the light of modern day, yet still make for a lifesaving tactical lesson for both the old hands and the whippersnappers of the 21st Century.

Revolvers and some semi-autos such as ones without grip safeties are capable of being fired upside down in fake surrender positions, or quickly flipped into a conventional handgrip. These moves were once passed on and practiced by both the enforcement and the criminal class. You obviously still can find these six-shooters today and certainly many still in the hands of the bad guys — who buy them or steal them.

Seeing the photos on the pages of this book we can all make cool-headed deductions, but in the heat of a raid, the sudden catch of a burglar, a simple arrest, or faced with multiple opponents, we may misread the false surrender under stress. Don't let this happen to you. Pass it on!

The Classic Pistol Rollover

This is classic pistol rollover. You confront the criminal and he makes a hands-up sign of surrender. He virtually points his barrel at himself, offering you to step up and seize the empty handle. He may be voicing cowardice, quivering words. Then suddenly when you look at his face, or anywhere else other than the gun? He rolls up that pistol in his hand faster than you can imagine, faster than you expected such a thing could be done. This move may also be done with certain semi-automatics. A good gunman knows what he can and cannot do with his piece. Work on yours. Study others. You may need this trick to fool a criminal or an enemy soldier drawing down on you.

The Stagecoach Roll

Handle out and upside down. A rollover of the weapon with a outside flick of the wrist gets the gun in firing position.

The Upside Down Shoot

Practice shooting with your pistol upside down. Your enemy does.

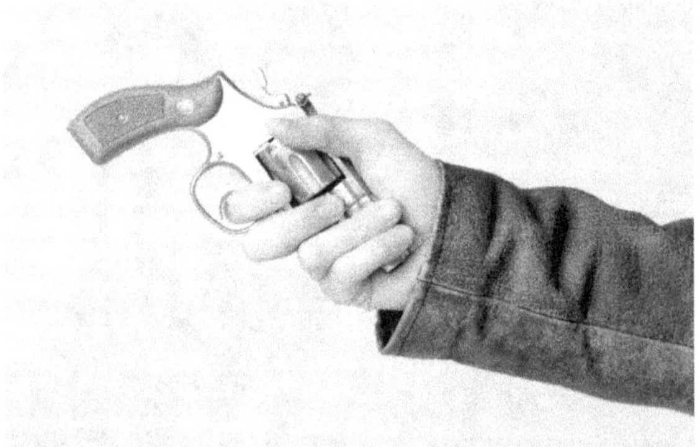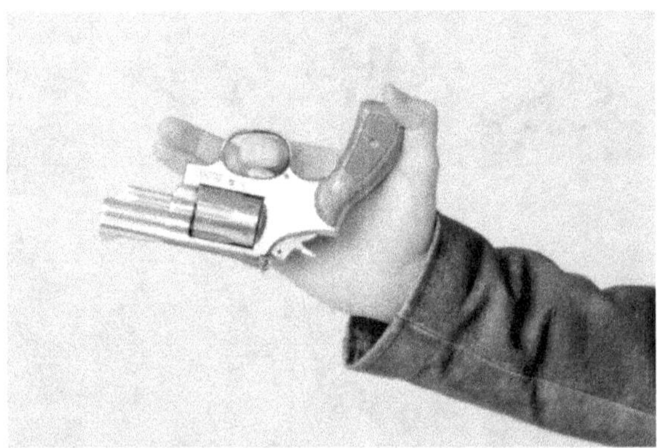

This is surely a surrender position? Not really. Let the weapon fall forward. With a torque of a wrist, the pistol handle can seat against the ball of the thumb. Many pistols may be fired upside down. Semi-automatics with grip safeties need their safeties depressed.

This is surely a surrender position? But not really. If the suspect lets the weapon fall forward, or even backward with a sudden torque of a wrist, the pistol handle can seat against the ball of the thumb. This braces for a trigger pull. Many pistols may be fired upside down, and professionals usually practice doing so once in a while on the range, testing different trigger pulls and weapons.

Many of today's semi-automatic handguns have grip safeties and require these safeties to be depressed with a conventional handhold. Recently I tried to shoot an old revolver upside down and could not muster enough pinky strength to discharge the weapon! But, as shown above, the trigger finger may be doing the work even upside down.

Quick Checklist of the Characteristics of Detecting Armed Opponents

Remember the common weapon carry sites:

Carry Site 1) Primary: Think quick draw.
Carry Site 2) Secondary: Think back-up weapon.
Carry Site 3) Tertiary: Think lunge and reach.
Learn) The hand pathways to these sites.

1) Approximately 90 percent of the world's population is right-handed.

2) Most firearms are carried on their dominant hand side.

3) Most are carried on or around the waistband, jacket and pants pockets.

4) Most are concealed from easy view. This causes the wearing of extra clothing, even in hot weather.

5) Guns in jacket pockets create unusual weight causing stretch and swing visual clues.

6) The butt, barrel or general shape of the weapon often leaves an impression of its shape on this clothing.

7) In cold weather, a criminal may wear a glove only on his non-gun hand.

8) Why does this person have the hip or fanny pack? Is there already a wallet in his pocket?

9) Most carriers must modify their body movements to compensate the extra weight and size.

10) Carriers frequently touch and manipulate these guns to reposition them, or feel more confident.

11) Most press the weapon against their body when running, just moving fast or sometimes when bending.

12) Carriers may also utilize straps, slings, wraps, string, wire, or Velcro to facilitate the concealment.

13) Most criminals do not use holsters.

14) Despite the exotic and tricky designs of zip guns, lighter guns, wallet guns, etc., all must have a muzzle of some type.

15) Many will use theatrics to distract you.

16) Watch out for sudden bend-overs, lean-overs, and turns.

17) Watch out for a subject who is scanning the area for witnesses or accomplices.

18) Watch the hands. It's the hands that will reach for weapons and kill you.

19) Try not to let multiple opponents separate too far and possibly surround you.

20) If a weapon is discovered during a search? Don't stop there. Keep searching.

Your gun is out and pointed at the subject. Your command presence performance is in full swing, punctuated by the barrel of your firearm. He has no weapon in his hands, yet he may go for one from on or around him? That is one legitimate reason to have your weapon trained on him.

But in the end, the presentation of a firearm upon an unarmed man and your commands for him to obey, really turn out to be little more than a implied bluff that you will shoot him if he doesn't respond. You can't shoot an unarmed man as a rule, whether he just stands there or simply runs away.

So, there you are standing before him with your threats and your pistol, and, he charges. This happens with some regularity for a host of reasons. The criminal thinks you are not man enough to pull the trigger. Or he knows the law and knows you can't and won't shoot him. Or, in an senseless, disjointed, instantaneous decision, he foolishly loses his logic and for that specific moment in time doesn't care what happens to him. Or, he has planned a "suicide by cop," or a suicide by soldier or civilian.

If you are civilian, you may shoot in self defense. But, inexperienced fools with guns will declare all kinds of simplistic, macho epitaphs about "...shooting the bastard." It's ignorant talk. It is just not that simple. The totality of the circumstances will dictate if you will survive the grand jury, even the criminal and civil jury, least of all the rush of a wounded madman.

If you are a soldier in the middle of a hot war, you probably can shoot. If that same soldier is on a foot beat of a police action, he might not be able to, fearing a political nightmare.

If you are a diminutive women shooting at a large bald, cursing, charging lunatic, you should survive the process.

If you are the huge, muscle-bound, hulk shooting at a 5 foot tall, unarmed skinny teen running at you? They will wonder why you shot him and did not swat him aside.

If you are an enforcement official you'd better not shoot, at least not at that precise second! A second later, he is on you and maybe grabbing for your gun. At this exact point, even a common person/juror may begin to understand that should that criminal get your gun from you, he may well shoot you with it.

It comes down to this. The law in general will not allow you to shoot a man running at you. Prosecutors, judges and juries may expect you instead to use, spray, or a baton, or empty hands. Yet, the law may allow you to shoot a man actively in-the-clutches-fighting with you over your gun. It is important you understand this distinction, a distinction of just a few feet and a second, changes the complexion of the situation.

In truth, the response here requires a sophisticated check and balance evaluation, all in an instant. A licensed concealed carry citizen, a police officer and a soldier must have a working knowledge of less-than-lethal responses in this situation. Their training doctrine must adequately cover the possibilities. You must be prepared to articulate that you understand the issues involved.

Why They Run at You:
1) The criminal thinks you are not man enough to pull the trigger.
2) He knows the law and knows you can't and won't shoot.
3) In an instant's decision, he foolishly loses his senses and doesn't care what happens to him.
4) He has planned a "suicide by cop" departure.

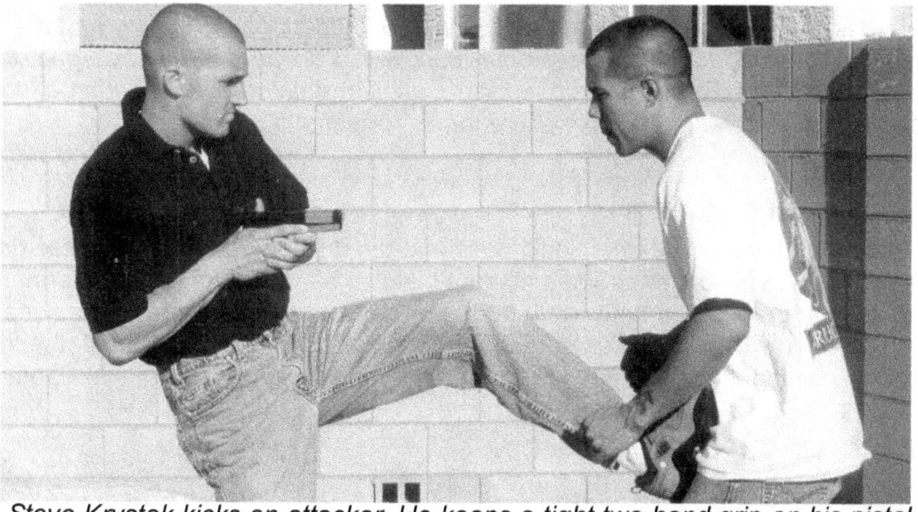

Steve Krystek kicks an attacker. He keeps a tight two-hand grip on his pistol.

Blasphemed as "pistol-whipping" decades ago by ignorant, desk bound administrators, people forgot the life-saving aspects of clubbing an attacker with a handgun rather than shooting him. Yet, modern day pragmatics like Las Vegas Metro Officer and Former Military SWAT commander Steve Krystek have resurrected the smarter, tactical aspects of the lost science of the pistol strike-using the several pounds of metal in your hand as an impact weapon against a rushing unarmed attacker. He has created a course on the subject.

Pistol striking work-out overview:
Stand before a heavy bag, or a training partner with a kicking shield or pad. With a replica pistol, start pounding:

The Variables:
> Right hand grip
> Left hand grip
> Two hand, right pistol grip primary
> Two-hand, left pistol grip primary

The Strikes:
> Downward strikes
> Upward strikes
> Right side strikes
> Left side strikes
> Thrusting strikes

Practice the UC kicks while holding a pistol.
Review Level 4's pistol retention skills.
Review Level 6's malfunction clearance skills.

Contact Krystek at www.PFCTraining.com for this and all manner of combat firearm training.

(name withheld)

The Block, Pass and Pin Re-Holster Drill

By now all readers should be familiar with the block, pass and pin drill, one depicted in these books since *Training Mission One.* In this version, the trainee holds a pistol in his hand versus an unarmed trainer. The trainer charges, crashing into the trainee and both work the block, pass and pin pattern. The trainee blocks as in a beat one, passes as in a beat two, and pins as in beat three. On beat three-and-one-half, the trainee pushes on the upper arm and body, gaining the space needed to re-holster the weapon. This is a skill, practice drill, not a scenario.

The block of an attack. The trainee passes the rushing arm. Then the trainee pushes the trainer hard. He re-holsters to fight the unarmed man with his empty hands, or use spray, or baton, or whatever is appropriate.

Pistol Strike! The Outside Invasion Series

Outside-to-outside-arm contact is made!

All too often, an armed person is confronted by an unarmed subject who still charges, despite the gun barrel threat. The military may still shoot in wartime combat situations. The police officer probably cannot. The civilian may, but this action may be proven wrong by criminal or civil courts. One solution is to strike the opponent with your handgun. In this series, we learn probable options for when the unarmed man charges.

Fearing the loss of your weapon should the opponent stun you and capture it, your goal is to strike the carotid with the butt of your pistol. He strikes out at you, tries to grab you, or tries to push you, and your weapon-bearing arm has made harsh contact with his arm. You will smash at his elbow area with your free hand, and try the strike.

From this point, the training series is set up this way:

Option 1: Your pistol strike lands on the carotid.

Option 2: The enemy blocks your incoming strike about half-way, or near the center of his body.

Option 3: The enemy grabs your gun-side forearm.

Option 4: The enemy over blocks your strike, or it crosses his center-line.

You smack down on the elbow area of his arm with your empty hand.

The Invasion Practice Set

The Set-Up
You crash/clash outside arm to outside arm. You palm strike his elbow freeing your pistol hand to strike his neck with the bottom of the pistol handle, or the bottom of the pistol frame.

Option 1: He fails to block.
Your gun strike lands on the carotid. The opponent does not block. This stunned or even knocked out the opponent. Holster your weapon and take the appropriate action as per your mission.

Option 2: He blocks half-way.
The enemy blocks your incoming strike about half-way, or near the center of his body. He doesn't grab yet, but barely gets a hand up. You elbow strike the forearm. Open your free hand and use the strike momentum to clear the hand from your weapon arm. Continue the strike. Finish as needed.

Option 3: He grabs your wrist.
The enemy grabs your gun-side forearm. Go for the quick joint lock release. Swing your elbow over the arm, twisting his hand grip. Then drive your elbow downward over the arm. You might also bend at the knees to help the force. Continue with the strike.

Option 4: He over-blocks.
The enemy over blocks your strike, or it crosses his center-line. This move requires some athletic savvy, but I have seen countless students acquire the skill with practice. And, it is not unlike some sports skills involved in football, baseball or basketball. You intercept his hand! You pull back. His block still travels forward. Your free hand scoops up the block, grabs and pulls it. You strike.

This is the best book I have read to date on this subject. It is not just for cops! Anyone who tries to thwart an enemy soldier or criminal may face this situation.

It is available from Looseleaf Law Publications, 43-08 162nd Street, Flushing, New York 11358

www.Looseleaflaw.com
800-647-5547

The Outside Invasion Series: Gun

Step 1) Defeating the contact arm.

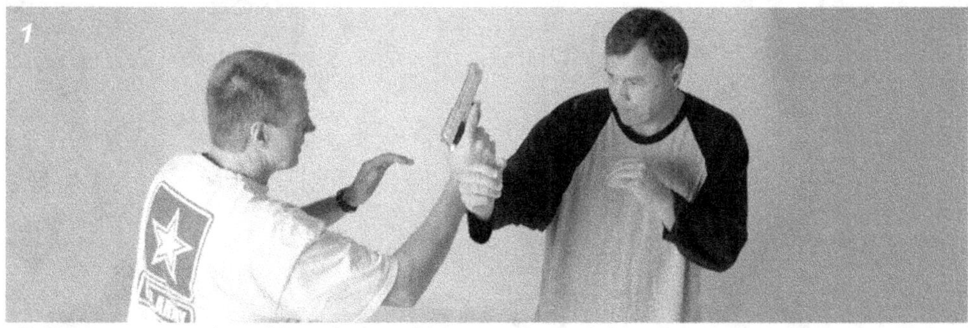

1) He is unarmed and he charges! You make outside-arm to outside-arm contact.

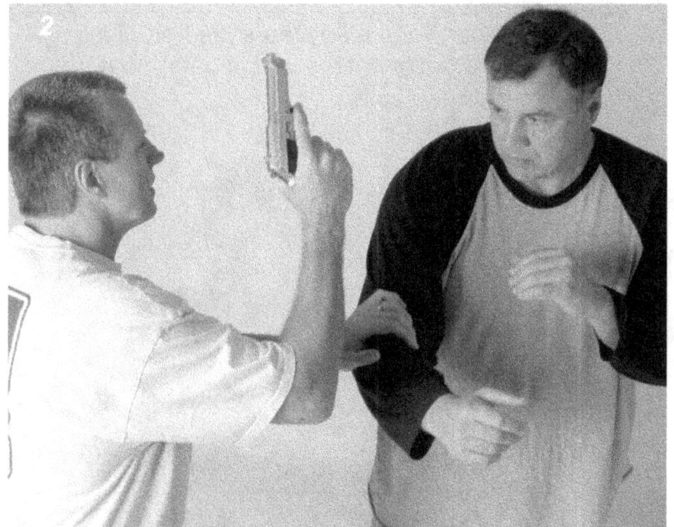

2) You slap his arm clear at the elbow.

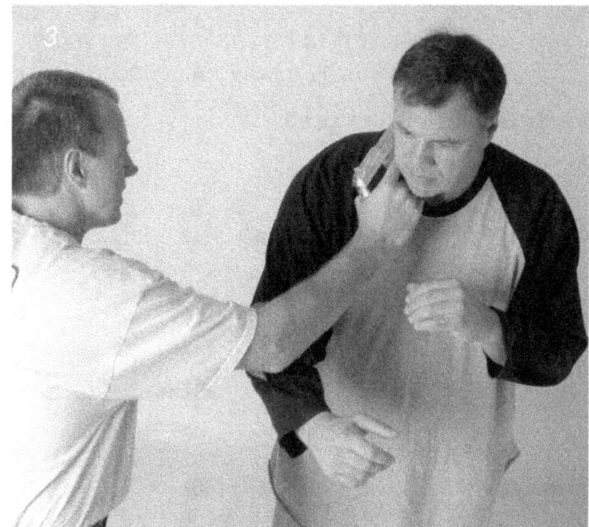

3) In this open path, the pistol strikes.

Step 2) Defeating the half-block.

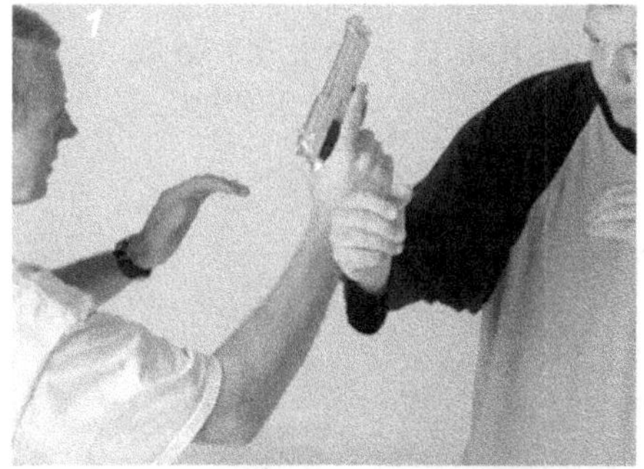

1) Outside contact.
2) You slap the arm clear on the elbow area. You try to strike.
3) His other hand blocks about half way, or to his center-line. No grab.

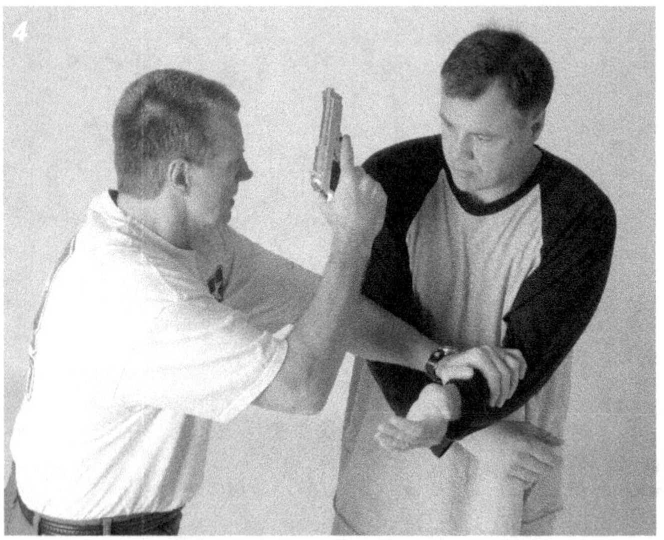

4) Your elbow strikes the first arm, pinning it. Drive forward in a powerful charge.

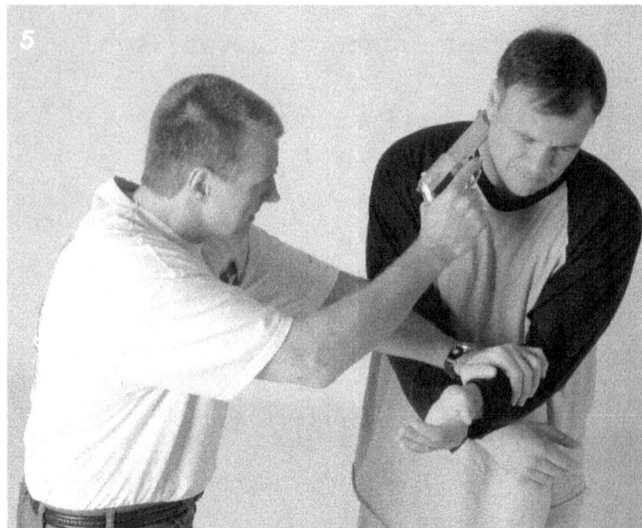

5) Your hand also clears his half-block. The pistol strikes in this open path.

Step 3) Defeating the grab.

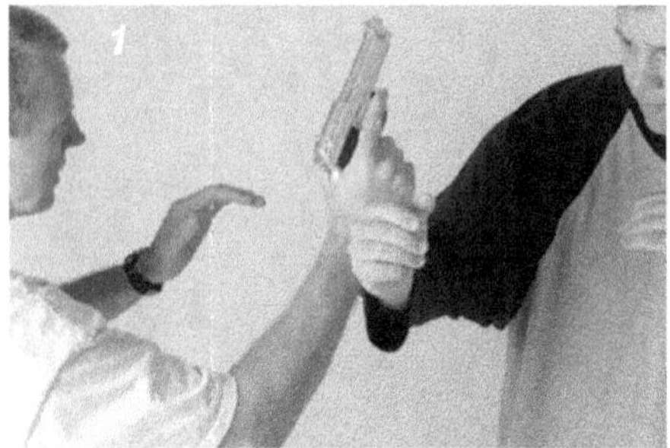

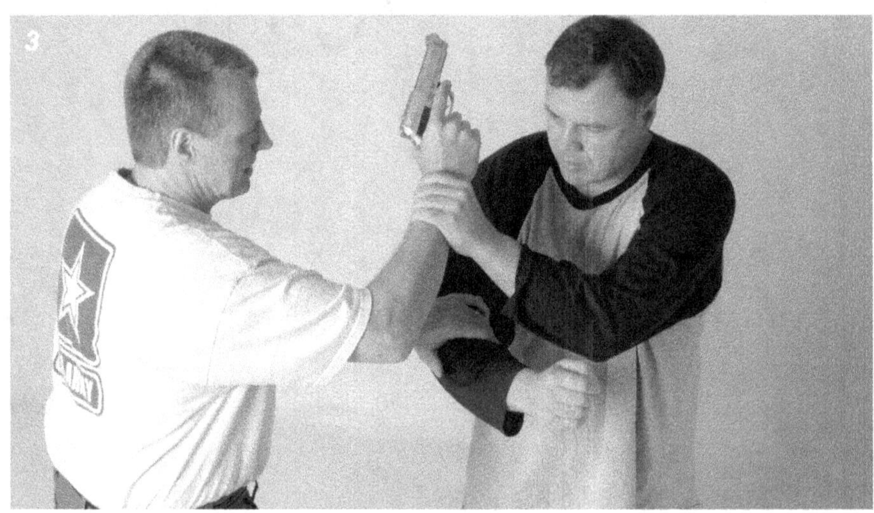

1) Outside contact.
2) You slap the arm clear on the elbow area. You try to strike.
3) His other hand comes over to block and grab your attempt.

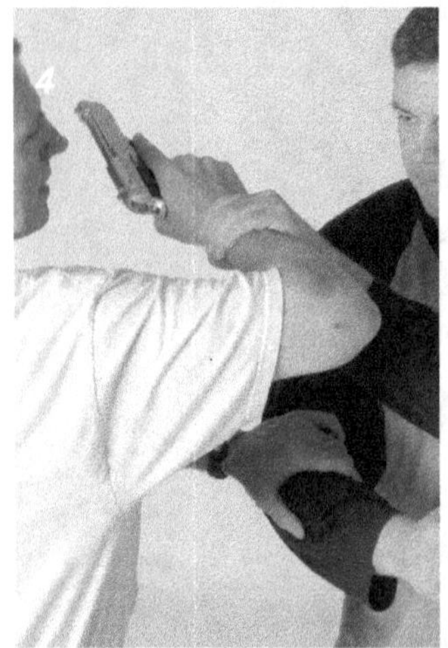

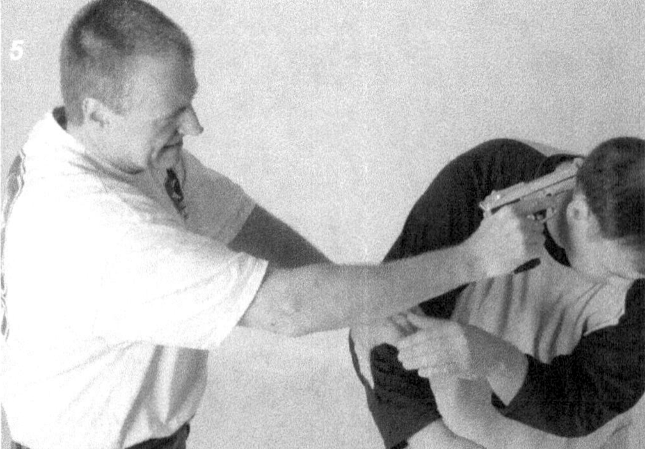

4) You roll your elbow over his arm and strike it downward. This releases his grip by attacking his wrist.

5) Strike in the suspect with your newly freed hand.

Step 4) Defeating the over-block.

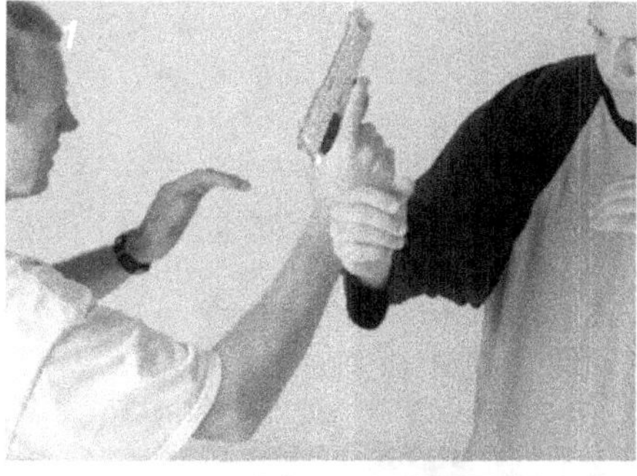

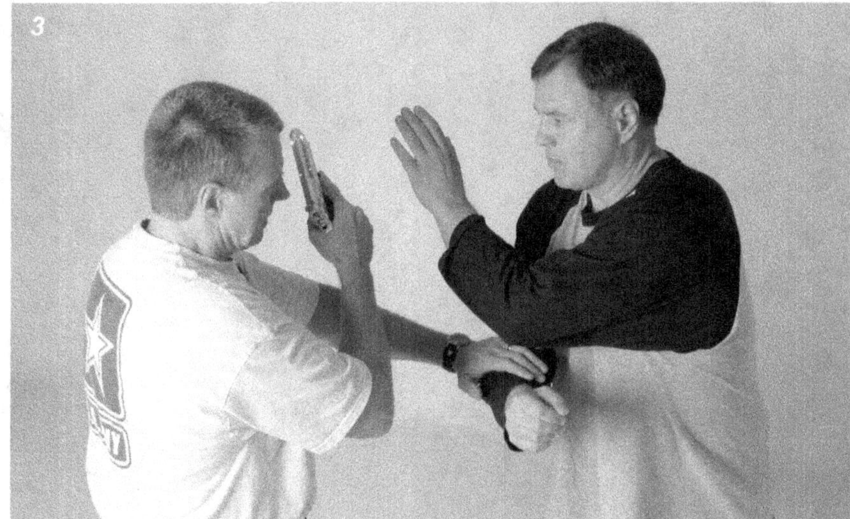

1) Outside contact.
2) You slap the arm clear on the elbow area. You try to strike.
3) His other hand anticipates this strike and over-blocks.

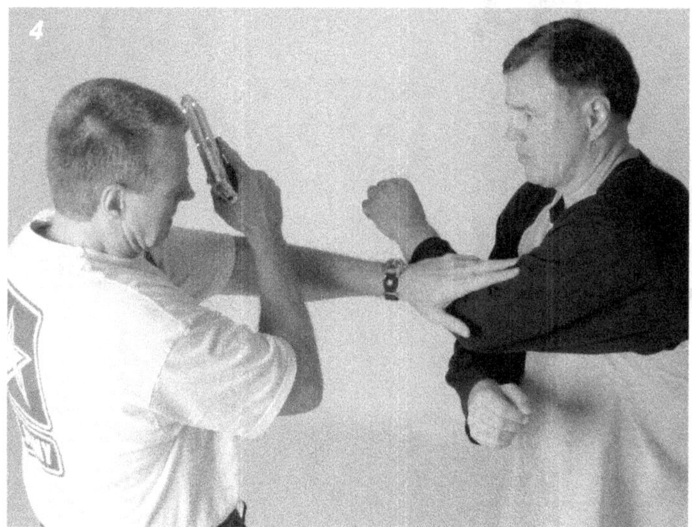

4) Your pinning hand circles up, hooks and
pins his over-blocking arm. Push down!

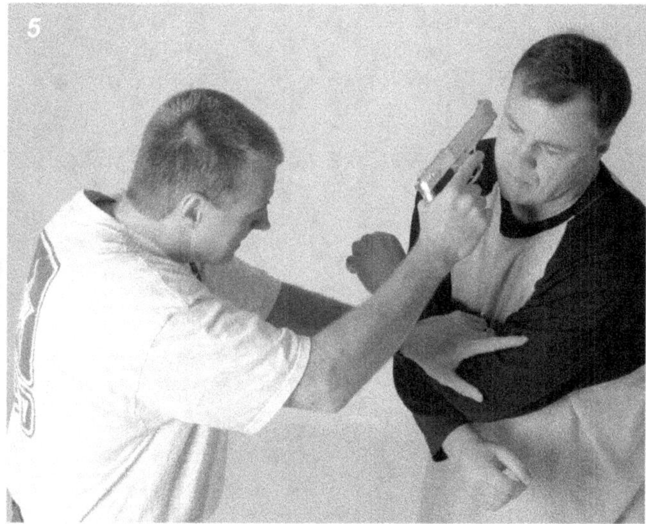

5) You strike in the opening.

The Hand Switch

Many respected professionals really dislike the use of a pistol as an impact weapon. They fear accidental discharges and the weapon being knocked out of battery in the scuffle.

They have developed methods to avoid the tactic. Veteran and respected instructor Ralph Mroz is a proponent of the hand switch to take the gun out and away from the unarmed, charging opponent. This frees up the strong-side hand for combat.

Ralph and London, England Metropolitan Officer James Sutherland demonstrate a hand switch scenario. In the situation, Ralph holds an unarmed man at bay when suddenly the man ignores the gun and charges at him.

Ralph begins the hand switch.

This switch frees his strong side hand for a power palm strike on the man's center line.

Here Ralph demonstrates the steps involved in the "no-shoot, "hand switch. The hand switch is easily practiced and easily performed. The trigger finger does not enter into the trigger guard. The weapon is accepted into the weak hand with a tight, secure grip.

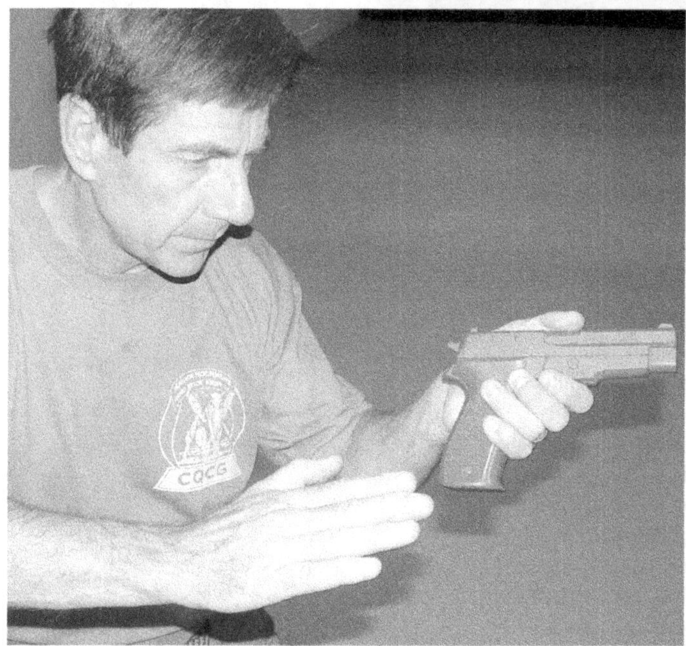

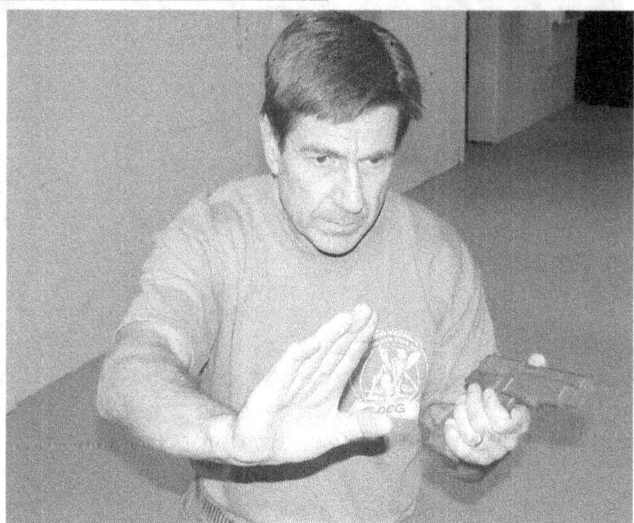

Studies and Observations 11) Searching Time?

Is it time to search the enemy? Beware! Whether an enforcement officer or a citizen, if you have captured a criminal there are some serious and ever-changing laws about searching suspects, rules that could ruin your career or cost you thousands in lawsuits. And to compound the confusion, each jurisdiction may have different rules. The classic tip, "consult with your local authorities..." on these problems is always advisable. One rule never changes. Your safety and the safety of others around you is the major justification to search a suspect.

So, you've got him in your aim, he seems to be cooperating and responding to your commands. But, you think he is armed with a weapon? Is there a need to search this very second? Can you wait for help for the proper authorities? Or backup?

If you can wait, and should he listen to your orders, you have commanded him to lie face down on the ground, arms and legs out.

If you must search, here is some advice. We'll start with what NOT to do. An old method was to completely search a suspect, then handcuff them. Even raw, green recruits such as myself decades ago could easily see that the longer the suspect's hands were free during this lengthy search process, grave danger existed. In our training sessions, drill instructors would hide weapons on their person, and no matter what clever *hands-behind-their head finger grabs*, or other tricks they taught us, a dedicated attacker would always get his hidden knife out and stab us in a split-second, while we searched him. There was no safe way to do this against a dedicated attacker. It seemed foolish not to secure the hands first, then search. Eventually, such a method became standard practice, but it took years to change in most countries. This is still doctrine in unenlightened countries.

Another near extinct search is the *wall search!* Photos of the infamous wall search are still lingering in old TV shows, movies, police and military textbooks and may confuse new readers. Throw these books away! In the infamous wall search, the suspect's palms are on the wall and his feet are far enough back that he is on an extended lean. This is supposed to keep him off balance while he is searched. In the 1970's it became apparent that prison inmates were practicing methods to defeat the standard wall search with several practical, effective escapes and counter-attack the administrating officers. The most common was to drop to the ground and wrap up the officer's legs for a takedown. Still, the wall search permeated doctrine for another decade until finally it was admonished in most countries. I sadly report that the wall search is still being taught in some countries.

Today, most officers handcuff their subjects as quickly as possible, then first search the body area accessible around the cuffed hands. Only then do they conduct a search around the rest of the body, with a heavy emphasis on the aforementioned primary, secondary and tertiary weapon carry sites.

We cuff or tie hands behind their backs for many reasons. Hands to front offer him easy double-fisted and forearm attacks, the ability to choke and strangle, and allow his hands near front pockets for potential concealed weapons or lock picks. He can remove his belt for an extended range weapon, and simply by lifting his hands to his chin, he can run rather fast.

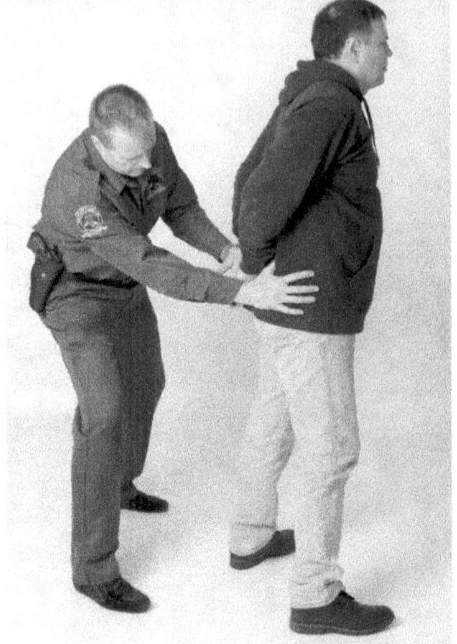

Search around the cuffed area first.

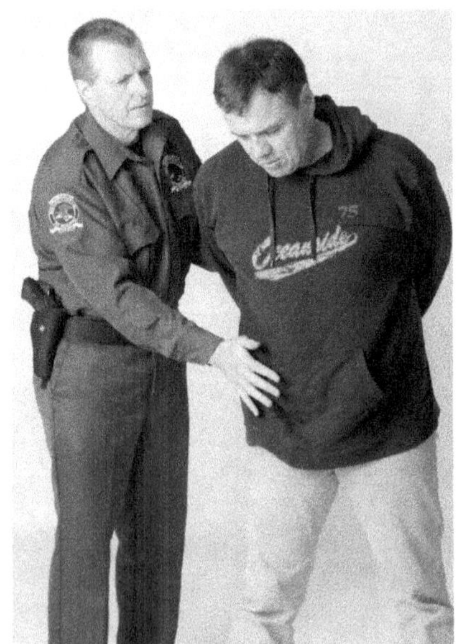

The pat down method.

The devious mind will work to outwit you. There are encyclopedias on how the bad guys hide their weapons in, on and around their bodies and continue to invent devices that do not appear to be weapons at first, but are deadly.

Search in a scientific, systematic manner so that you will not overlook a body part. Do not forget to search the groin area. The FBI reports that 70 percent of interviewed convicts reveal that the groin is the most overlooked body area when they have been searched. At one police agency I worked in, a rather large female was famous for concealing a snub nose revolver up her vagina-barrel up!

A patting of the body and/or a crushing method are two popular ways to search for weapons. Find a weapon? Where do you put it? The answer is situational. I once disarmed a knife from a drugged burglar. I was absolutely sure he and I were alone and pitched the long kitchen knife across the room. I knew instinctively that had I shoved the knife in my belt line, any subsequent fighting with this subject might cause the secured knife to stab my leg.

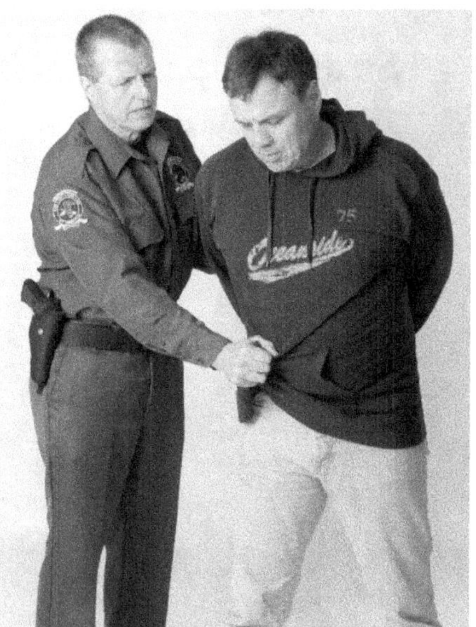

The hand crush method.

Suspects often carry needles. In some parts of the world, criminals use needles like knives to threaten their victims. When you use the pat down or crush methods be aware of this possibility. In some circumstances, officers carry the blunt EMT/medical scissors to cut open pockets and clothing parts for searching, not just when they suspect dangerous objects like needles, but also to open up secret pockets created for drug trafficking and other devious plans.

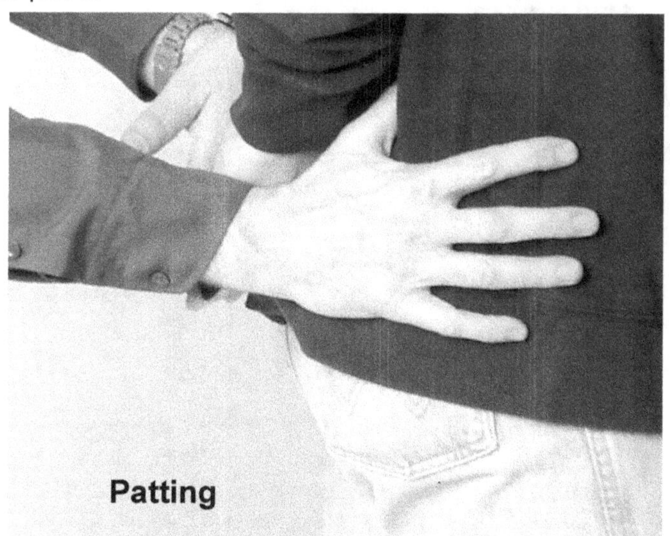

Patting

Crushing

Search Point 1) Keep abreast of changing laws.
Search Point 2) The time factor! Need to search? Can you wait for help?
Search Point 3) No Wall search!
Search Point 4) Cuff as soon as possible, then search areas around hands.
Search Point 5) Don't forget to search groin area.
Search Point 6) Search in a systematic manner.
Search Point 7) Pat and and crush methods
Search Point 8) The devious mind will work to outwit you. There are encyclopedias...
Search Point 9) Recovered weaponry? Knives? Guns? Where do you put them?
Search Point 10) Needles, a regional and global problem.
Search Point 11) EMT scissors-for safe cutting removal of suspect materials.

Spotting a hidden handgun

ASYMMETRICAL GAIT

A gun in a right-hand pocket or tucked into the right side of a waistband may hinder leg movement on that side, making the right stride shorter than the left.

A slightly clipped arm swing may also signal a hidden gun: the forearm on the gun side will tend to stay close to the body, instinctively guarding the weapon.

UPPER BODY SHIFT

When approached from the front, a person with a hidden gun will instinctively turn the gun side of his body away from the person approaching, and may veer to that side to avoid a face-to-face encounter. He is also likely to pull his arm in toward his body on the gun side.

A QUICK ADJUSTMENT

A gun's weight is distributed unevenly, with more of its weight in the grip than in the barrel. Vertical motion — like descending stairs or stepping onto a curb — tends to shift the barrel upward. A quick, circular movement of the hand or forearm adjusts the gun's position.

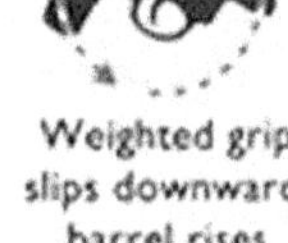

RUNNING FROM THE RAIN

When running toward shelter from rain, or across a busy street, a person concealing a gun is likely to brace the weapon with an arm or hand.

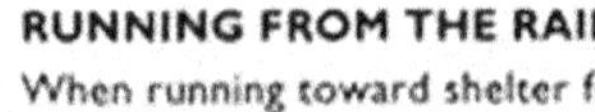

CONSPICUOUS CLOTHING

Garments worn to conceal weapons often appear odd, mismatched, or out of season, and can actually draw attention to a person trying to avoid scrutiny. A closer look may reveal movements or other characteristic signs of a hidden handgun.

JACKET FITS UNEVENLY
One side hangs lower than the other, and swings like a pendulum with each step

HAND RESTS ON GUN
Hand constantly feels for gun through clothing

HOLSTER BULGES
A holstered gun appears as a lump when arms are extended or when the body bends at the waist

STYLES DON'T MATCH
Oversized or mismatched coat seems incompatible with other clothing

CLOTHES DON'T SUIT WEATHER
A coat is open in cold weather, for quick access to a gun ... ...or closed in hot weather, to conceal one

Source: Robert T. Gallagher, former detective, Anti-Robbery Tactical Unit, New York City Police Department

Megan Jaegerman

Your Level 3 Gun/Counter-Gun Workout
Practice:

Pistol striking work-out overview:
Stand before a heavy bag, or a training partner with a kicking shield or pad. With a replica pistol, start pounding out:
- Downward strikes
- Upward strikes
- Right side strikes
- Left side strikes
- Thrusting strikes

The Chase Drill
The trainee pulls a variety of props as he turns, to include handguns to coach the trainee's responses.

- utilize the "false surrender" and "is he dead yet" drills.
    * include unarmed charges and the Outside Invasion Series."

- conduct searches of a suspect. The trainer may hide weapons.

- finish with the Arrest Process.

Lauric would like to thank the following for their time and support in the production of this book.

Tom Barnhart
Steve Krystek
Jeff Laun
Ralph Mroz
Randy Roberson
James Sutherland
Jerry VanCook
Ronnie Young

Photography by:

Jane Eden

Edited by:

Jane Eden
Thomas Pentzer